Pearl Jam

Editor: **Mike Evans**
Production Controller: **Michelle Thomas**
Picture Research: **Emily Hedges**
Art Editor: **Ashley Western**
Design: **Design Revolution**

First published in 1994 by
Hamlyn, an imprint of
Reed Consumer Books Limited,
Michelin House, 81 Fulham Road,
London SW3 6RB
and Auckland, Melbourne, Singapore and Toronto

A Catalogue record for this book is available from the British Library
ISBN 0-600-58426-7

Printed in Spain by Cayfosa. Barcelona

Picture Acknowledgements

London Features International: 7 bottom left, 9, 56, 69, 70 top right Kristin
Callahan: 50, 51 Kevin Mazur: 69 below top and above centre;

Melody Maker: 21 right, 38 right, 39 left and right, 59 top right and top left, 60 top
left Steve Gullick: 4, 12, 15, 25, 28, 33, 34-35, 36 top and bottom, 37, 41, 42 top
and bottom, 43 top and bottom, 45, 48-49, 52, 59 top right, 61 Phil Nicholls: 44
Charles Peterson 24 Tom Sheehan 64 bottom, 66 top left and bottom left, 66-67
top and bottom, 67 top right and bottom righl Kevin Westenburg 6;

Pictorial Press: 55, Mayer: 62-63, 69 bottom, 70 top left, left of centre and
bottom, 71 top right, right of centre and bottom Star File/Bob Leafe: 30 top Star
File/Pulin: 54;

Redferns: Mick Hutson: 14 Michel Linssen: 47 top right, right of centre, top left
and left of centre Susan Moore: 46 bottom;

Retna: Dave Alloca: 38 left Matt Anker: 3,13, 27 top Jay Blakesberg: 47 bottom
Anthony Gordon: 10-11, 30 bottom, 32, 80 background Eddie Malluck 26 Neal
Preston: 22, 60 bottom, 80 inset RIP 27 bottom, 69 below centre Chris Taylor: 58
Neils van Iperen: 18-19 Scott Weiner 23;

Rex Features: Dave Hogan: 65 bottom LGI/Jim Graham: 29 left and right
LGI/Steve Jennings: 46 top, 53 right LGI/Van Martin: 75, 79;

Kyle Shelley: 31;

S.I.N.: 20-21, 59 bottom left and bottom right Anita Bugge: 7 top right, top left
and bottom right, 8 Greg Freeman: 17, 72 Jana 5, 40, 53 left, 64 top, 65 top, 68,
73, 74 top left, top right, bottom left and bottom right, 76-77, 78 left and right
Roy Tee 57;

Warner Brothers: Michael Levine: 19 bottom right;

Pearl Jam

ALLAN JONES

HAMLYN

CONTENTS

Cracking Up   5

Like A Hurricane   9

Seattle Be The Day   17

Say Hello 2 Heaven   25

Counting To Ten   33

Trouble Waiting   57

The Satanic Versus   61

World Leader Pretend   73

Cracking Up

NOW that you happen to ask, this is what Eddie Vedder has to say about exactly what happened on that now-notorious afternoon in Denmark at the Roskilde rock'n'roll festival, where by all accounts he flipped out so badly that if he hadn't gone quietly they might have had to take him back home to Seattle in a straitjacket.

Eddie Vedder's stage-diving, crowd-surfing, call it what we will, gave a whole new meaning to the idea of audience participation

'You take a block of ice,' he says, 'and you hold it under hot running water and what happens? It cracks. That show, I cracked.'

When you went on stage, what sort of state were you in?

'Just... bad. Like, "Someone get me through this." I don't think any of us wanted to be there.' This is Pearl Jam bassist Jeff Ament. 'It was pretty intense. I remember sitting in the dressing room and it was really weird.

What brought on all this weirdness?

'The day before, we played in Stockholm,' Eddie Vedder recalls. 'Great show. I remember there wasn't an opening act, so we had one of the crew go on and pretend to play a Bob Marley song. I was standing behind some amps, playing acoustic guitar and singing. Everyone thinks it's him, the crew guy, they fall for it hook, line and sinker. Then I come out, play a couple of songs and then the band comes out and it goes really

well. We play for a couple of hours. It feels great. We tell the audience we're gonna play until it gets dark. Which is a joke, of course, because at that time of the year in Sweden it doesn't get dark. It doesn't even get dusk.

'Anyway, it's a good show. The audience is great, the whole feeling is great. It's one of those shows where you end up feeling you've really shared something with the audience. It's a really happening thing, you know. And then we get backstage, and Dave the drummer says, "Hey, I think my bag's missing." We say, "Hey, be cool. Don't worry, you'll find it." And then I start looking around and my shit is missing.

'The main things I'm missing are, like, two school composition books. One had all kinds of lyrics in it, and the other . . . well, it was real personal. See, I never finished high school. So I guess I've had to educate myself. I learn about geography, language

and history while I'm travelling and I write down what I learn in these notebooks.

CONFUSION

'They're no big deal to anyone else. But they mean a fucking lot to me, man. It was real personal shit, you know. And someone walks in while we're playing and steals 'em. Some fucking asshole just walks in and steals 'em. That was it for me. That was what cracked me up. The stuff that was stolen was just irreplaceable. I said, 'I'm fucking outta here. I'm not around.' You're on stage, you know, and you think you're giving everything you've got – but there's always someone who wants more. And if you can't give it, they'll just fucking take it.'

So you get to Roskilde the next day, and what happens? I heard you were trying to get closer to the audience or something and ended up swapping punches with the festival security.

'Oh, that,' Eddie Vedder laughs.

Is it true?

'Yeah . . . yeah. I guess so.'

Do you not want to talk about it?

'No . .uh. . It's actually quite interesting, because I hadn't really thought about any of this until you just brought it up.'

So what happened?

'Well, first of all, there's like thirty feet separating the stage and the crowd. And that was something I had a problem with. But despite this insane fucking distance, this one guy actually manages to get on the stage.

and they've got him in a headlock and they're pounding on him. And it's a bad fucking scene. I mean, these guys are really pounding him.

'So then I jump off the stage and jump them.

'And of course they think I've jumped in from the crowd. They don't know who the fuck I am. So suddenly we're all fighting. And I'm fucking livid. This shit isn't supposed to be happening. But here we all are. Fists flying. All these people fighting. And our tour manager's in there by now as well and in the confusion he almost hits a

spoke to *Melody Maker* to explain why you were pulling the shows, he said there was no alternative. If the band had just carried on, pretty soon there was going to be no more band.

FLIPPED

Was this an overreaction, or had things really got so badly out of hand?

'It really was a turning point for us,' Jeff says. 'It was the first time we admitted to ourselves that we really were tired and were about to lose control over what was happening. Up to that point, we'd pretty much kept our opinions about touring to ourselves. Up to that point, we'd always thought there was nothing we could really do, because these things are all planned out in advance and you end up feeling responsible for so many people – the record company, the crew, the fans. You think there's nothing you can do to stop it once it's all in motion.

'Looking back, though, we had no choice. We were just physically and spiritually exhausted. We had to come off the road. I really believe that if we hadn't taken a break, there would have been no more band.'

Eddie starts laughing, though neither Jeff nor I know why.

'I'm sorry,' he says, chuckling like a clacking hyena. 'I was just thinking of something . . . Do you remember that doctor or whatever he was who they sent to examine me? That's what I'm laughing at. Because we had to cancel those dates, I guess for insurance purposes or whatever, they needed someone to come in and have a look at me and kinda confirm to whoever that I really couldn't go on.

'So I'm sitting there like something out of Harold And Maud, and I realise that this guy wants to write down that I'm fucking crazy. So I thought, "OK, I'll give you crazy." And I start walking around the room, really freaking out. Gibbering. Kicking stuff over. Ranting and raving. I really gave him something to fucking diagnose.

'As far as he was concerned, there was no question about it. I'd fucking flipped. I was fucking crazy, man. I was gone.'

Rock solid mainstay of Pearl Jam in more ways than one, bass player Jeff Ament

It's just amazing. Incredible. The fact that he can get through that amount of security! I mean, that guy wins. That guy gets a prize. And to top it all, he does this amazing dive off the stage. Hey! Give him another prize. He deserves it. But what he actually gets is a pretty solid fucking beating.

'He jumps off the stage and, like, six guys – these six overzealous guys who've probably been watching too much American Football or something – they jump on him

woman. So I have to haul off on him. It was crazy.'

So basically, you lost control?

'I'm always losing control.'

But you get it back?

'Sooner or later, yeah,' he laughs uncomfortably. 'I'm always losing control and getting it back.'

After what happened in Roskilde, you cancelled the London shows that were scheduled for the following week. When Jeff

★★★★★★★★★★★★★★★★

Like A Hurricane

No One Surfs Forever

YOU wonder just what would have happened to the young Eddie Vedder if the rock 'n' roll scene generally and Pearl Jam specifically hadn't come along when it did, to completely revolutionize his life and make his aching teenage dreams come true.

If things had turned out differently, if the connections that eventually led him to Pearl Jam hadn't been made, where would he have ended up, and in what sort of state?

Given the feverish and urgent pulse of his obsession, you can only suppose that without music his life would have been meaningless, an unfocused drift. You can imagine him in San Diego, struggling with a series of dead-end jobs in the dreary routine of low-income employment, always at someone's beck and holler, sinking into the desolation of unrealised dreams and wrecked ambition, strung out on disappointment, drugs and the bad dreams of the nation, going nowhere, his entire life a sad catalogue of missed opportunities.

You wonder what he would have done for an audience then, and it's not difficult to imagine Eddie losing it badly, ending up like one of those people you run into on the indifferent streets of American cities, lashing out at passers-by with a bicycle chain, maybe, and gibbering oaths and ancient diatribes, barely comprehensible, a violent cackling full of phlegm and bile.

In the darkest desperate mood of his hopeless frustration, could he even perhaps have ended up as one of those people who for reasons no one can later understand gets up one morning and decides to take out their frustration with the world by walking into their local McDonald's with guns blazing You can see it all too clearly. Floors black with blood, bodies piled up in mounds, entire families, all that food, Nikes twitching in the American sunlight. Paramedics and TV crews arriving in a rush. Cops with shotguns already on the scene, cool seen-it-all-before professionals. And Eddie, handcuffed, is being taken into custody with a blanket over his head.

Or maybe he would have ended up joining one of America's increasingly popular fringe religious cults, an expert in explosives, small arms and apocalyptic texts, waiting for the end of the world and finally checking out in gunfire and a halo of flames.

These are extreme speculations. But when you think of Eddie, you can't help thinking like this. You think of Eddie and you naturally think of someone who's prepared to go all the way in whatever he might chose to do.

And whichever way you look at it, without music you can only imagine Eddie being fucked up in the biggest possible way.

IN THE NAME OF THE FATHER

''Music saved me,' he told interviewers, years later. 'I mean,' he would continue, 'my upbringing was like a hurricane, and music was the tree I held onto. That's how important it was, and is.

'That's why I fully vow to help people out with whatever comes my way . . . Because I went through the ice myself once or twice, you know.'

Eddie in action in Oslo, during the European visit of February 1992

to Michael Jackson records, and to this day when I pull out a record with the blue Motown logo of the map of Detroit on it, I get chills.'

In 1974, when Eddie was eight, the family moved to San Diego. It was a time of increasing tensions, including rows with his parents, unhappiness at school, trauma and resentment. Music was again a comfort and inspiration, a bandage for weeping wounds.

He was 13, and of all the music he listened to it was 'Quadrophenia', The Who's 1973 song cycle about England's lost and derelict young, that offered him most solace, that sustained him and reminded him that he wasn't alone in his adolescent agony.

'I was going through a really tough time, and the "Quadrophenia" album saved my life,' he confessed to *Rock Power* magazine in 1992. 'I thought it was so amazing that Pete Townshend, this guy who lived thousands of miles away in another country, could totally explain my life. It was really intense, and obviously I wasn't the only one who felt that way.'

BITTERNESS

Talking to *Melody Maker*'s Andrew Mueller in Oslo in February 1992, Eddie was even more explicit about the debt he owed Pete Townshend and The Who.

'I just kind of came to this realisation today that Pete Townshend was probably more of a father to me than anybody,' he said. 'And yet I never sent him a Father's Day card. I feel pretty guilty about that.'

For a long time after he became famous with Pearl Jam, Eddie was purposely vague about the circumstances of his upbringing that caused him such unhappiness, pain and anger at his family.

It wasn't until an interview in *Rolling Stone* in October 1993 that he elaborated upon this part of his past that was still a source of bitterness and regret.

'I never knew my real dad,' he told the writer and film maker Cameron Crowe. 'I had another father that I didn't get along with, a guy I thought was my father. There were fights and bad, bad scenes. I was kind of on

Eddie was born on December 23, 1966, in Evanston, Illinois, a northern suburb of Chicago. He was known as Eddie Mueller then, and he was the eldest of four boys. For a while, childhood was idyllic, a season of uncomplicated happiness. When he was five, however, his parents took charge of a group home for parentless children. The orphaned kids were a mix of Afro-Americans and Irish and could be pretty wild company.

'I went from being the oldest kid in my family, to being this little punk among all these bigger punks,' he would recall. 'All of a

sudden, most of my brothers were older, and black, and Irish. All these intense diverse cultures.'

Interviewers would want to know how he coped in this new environment.

'I learned how to box,' he would answer.

Being a lot older than Eddie, most of these kids were already into music, listening mostly to soul, R&B and Motown. 'Their musical tastes rubbed off on me,' Eddie would remember. 'That's when I got into Smokey Robinson, James Brown, Otis Redding, The Jackson Five. I started singing my own at a pretty young age.'

His parents decided to move back to Chicago when he was 15. He'd started to play in local bands and was determined to pursue a career in music. He announced that he was staying in San Diego. There was an acrimonious farewell to the man who Eddie would soon learn was his stepfather, and they haven't spoken since. Eddie had never got on well with him and they had never been close. It wasn't until a year later, however, when his mother flew out from Chicago to see him in San Diego that he came close to understanding what lay at the grim heart of his problems.

'She came out with the specific purpose to tell me that this guy wasn't my father,' Vedder told Cameron Crowe. 'I remember at the time I was like "I know he's not my father, he's a fucking asshole." And she said, "Oh, Eddie, he's *really* not your father." 'At first I was pretty happy about it, then she told me who my real dad was. I had met the guy three or four times, he was a friend of the family, kind of a distant friend. He later died of multiple sclerosis.

So when I met him, he was in the hospital. He had crutches, or maybe he was in a wheelchair.'

Years later, his mother's visit and the specific circumstances of her confession were vividly inscribed on his memory. He had forgotten nothing. 'There was a

piano in the room, and I remember really wishing I knew how to play a happy song. I was happy for about a minute, and then I came down. I had to deal with the fact that he was dead. My real father was not on this earth. I had to deal with the anger of not being told sooner, not being told while he was alive. I was a big secret. Secrets are bad news. Secrets about adoptions, any of that stuff. It's got to come out, don't keep it. It just gets bigger and darker and deeper and uglier and messy.'

What went down that day between Eddie and his mother would eventually be agonisingly recalled on Pearl Jam's 'Alive', which is credited

on the lyric sheet insert of 'Ten' to Edward Louis Severson III. Eddie's real father was Edward Louis Severson II, who is among the Pearl Jam family members to whom 'Ten' was dedicated. Edward Louis Severson II was a musician himself, it turned out, a singer and organist who sang in restaurants and hotel lounges.

RETROSPECTIVE

As soon as what had been kept secret from him for so long was out in the open, Eddie found himself surrounded by well-meaning, but often unwelcome relatives.

'There were all these things they wanted to say,' he told *Rolling Stone,* 'like, "*That's* where you got musical talent," and I was like, "Fuck you." At the time, I was 14 or 15, I didn't even know what the fuck was going on. I learned how to play guitar, saved all my money for equipment, and you're telling me that's where it came from? Some fucking broken-down old lounge act? Fuck you.'

Eddie, who adopted his mother's maiden name when he discovered the truth of his parentage, was not quick to reconcile himself with the way he thought he'd been hurt and deceived and prevented from ever really knowing his father. He blamed everyone, including himself, and wrapped himself in a retrospective pain. There is much at the heart of his music that still reflects his unsettled relationship with his family. 'They've given me a lifetime's worth of material to write about,' he noted with grim irony in his interview with Crowe.

With the passing of time, however, the turbulence of his upbringing and his relationship with his father was put in a more reasoned perspective. He learned to live with even the most uncomfortable memories.

'The strange thing is that there are so many similarities between my father and I,' he eventually admitted. 'He had no impact on my life, but here I am. I look just like him. People in my family – they can't help it – they look at me like I'm a replacement. That's where "Alive" comes in. But I'm proud of the guy now. I appreciate my heritage. I have a very deep feeling for him in my heart.

SURF'S UP

Perhaps in a spirit of reconciliation or maybe in belated recognition of his musical aspirations, which she only now began to take seriously, his mother's final gesture before flying back to Chicago was to buy him a guitar, a black 1980 Fender Telecaster. Eddie knew his limitations, however.

'I wasn't Jimi Hendrix and didn't know if I ever could be,' he said later, explaining why he soon decided that his most effective musical role would be as a singer. 'It just seemed like it was easier and more direct to just scream in somebody's face.'

Eddie played in a lot of bands during the next few years as the Eighties rolled into the Nineties. There were The Butts, for instance, and Surf & Destroy, and they played mostly punk and hardcore and never really seemed to get anywhere. Eddie refused to be discouraged, however, and never lost faith. If only he could hang on, something would happen. He would hear the call, and the things he'd dreamed about, longed for and wanted so desperately it hurt like a bruise, would actually become reality. Eddie was always a true believer.

By the beginning of the Nineties, however, he was at a low ebb. Bad Radio, his most recent band, had just split up. He was working nights, from midnight until eight in the morning, pumping gas in a San Diego petrol station. The shifts were long, but business at nights was usually slow, which gave him plenty of time to concentrate on his songwriting. When he got off work, he'd go down to the beach near Encinitas and surf. For Eddie, surfing was an experience almost as mystical as rock'n'roll.

'People think of sun and sand and girls, but surfing's not really like that,' he later explained. 'At eight in the morning, it's foggy and cold; you drag yourself into the ocean and you can't even see the waves through the fog. It's not very glamorous, but those are the best waves. The still water's like glass – you feel like you're breaking the plain for the first time as you're paddling out.

'It's a good time to think. Time alone is when you really connect with others, that's how their philosophies work, but I'm still trying to get in touch with myself. I've held my breath and swum as deep as I could down into myself, and then had to come up for air, or the pressure got too intense, my head felt like it was imploding.

'But I know I can go deeper, it's just a matter of holding my breath longer. I wanna hit the bottom of myself before I go hang out with a million other people.'

When the pounding surf had cleared his head, Eddie would go home and play guitar all day and work some more on his songs. In the early evening, he'd go down to one of his local clubs, sometimes Winter's on El Cajon Boulevard, where his longtime girlfriend Beth Leibling put on some shows, but more often the Bacchanal, where he had a part-time and usually unpaid job humping gear for bands. He'd hang out at soundchecks, stay on for the show, and at midnight go back to work for another eight hours. In San Diego, he was known as 'the guy who never slept'.

'I was a kind of mad scientist character,' Vedder told Andrew Mueller. 'People thought I'd either do really big things some day . . . or just die.'

One night at the Bacchanal club, Eddie worked as a casual roadie for Joe Strummer, the former Clash singer and guitar player who'd been recording a solo album called 'Earthquake Weather' in Los Angeles and was then doing a series of club dates to help knock the material for the new record into shape.

'I forewent my twenty-dollar paycheck that night just to hang out at soundcheck,' Eddie told Gina Arnold some time later, 'because to me, just to look at Joe Strummer's guitar was cool. I'd get chills just looking at it. And that night the power went off and I sat in a tiny room with Joe Strummer for, like, an hour with just this big mag light on his face. It was a totally surreal experience. I remember he gave me a hit off his cigarette and it was half pot and half tobacco, and I nearly puked . . . but of course you can't puke in front of your hero.'

Playing that night in Strummer's band was Jack Irons, the drummer with The Red Hot Chili Peppers. Jack and Eddie met and became best friends. They started to meet every Friday to play basketball and talk about music and just hang out together. One Friday in October 1990, Irons turned up for his weekly session with Eddie and after shooting a few baskets he gave him a tape of some songs that had been recorded by some people he knew in Seattle. These musicians were looking for a singer, Jack told Eddie. Perhaps Eddie would like to give it a listen, see what he thought, maybe even get in touch with these people up there in Seattle.

MINI-OPERA

Eddie took the tape home. It was labelled simply, 'STONE GOSSARD DEMOS'. There were five instrumental tracks on the tape and one of them especially caught Eddie's attention. It had a working title of 'Dollar Short', and it featured this great guitar bridge that after a while Eddie just couldn't get it out of his mind. It just kept running and running through his head, and somehow it brought to the surface a lot of the emotions that Eddie had kept suppressed for a long time.

One morning after work at the gas station, he was out surfing as usual in the early morning Encinitas mist with those riffs from 'Dollar Short' still playing in his head when the lyric for what would eventually become 'Alive' seemed to just come to him, almost unbidden.

He was soon back at Beth Liebling's apartment in Mission Beach where he taped himself singing over three of the instrumental tracks on Stone Gossard's demo tape. The trio of songs included 'Alive' and 'Once', both of which would appear on Pearl Jam's debut album, 'Ten', and an early version of 'Footsteps', which would eventually appear as one of the B-sides of the British single pressing of 'Jeremy'.

Norway falls to Pearl Jam, Oslo 1992

the father. You know how it is, first loves and stuff. And the guy *dies*. How could you ever get him back? But the son. He looks exactly like him. It's uncanny. So she wants *him*. The son is oblivious to it all. He doesn't know what the fuck is going on. He's still dealing, he's still growing up. He's still dealing with love, he's still dealing with the death of his father. All he knows is "I'm still alive" – those three words, that's totally out of burden.

KILLER

"Now the second verse is "Oh, she walks slowly into a young man's room . . . I can remember to this very day . . . the look . . . the look." And I don't say anything else. And because I'm saying "The look, the look", everyone thinks it goes with "on her face". It's not on her face. The look is between her *legs*. Where do you go with *that*? That's where you come from. 'But "I'm still alive". I'm the lover that's still alive. And the whole conversation about "You're still alive, she said". And his doubts: "Do I deserve to be? Is that the question?" Because he's fucked up forever! So now he doesn't know how to deal with it, so what does he do, he goes out killing people – that was "Once".

He becomes a serial killer. And "Footsteps", the final song of the trilogy, that's what happens when he gets executed. *That's what happens*. The Green River killer . . . and in San Diego, there was another prostitute killer down there. Somehow I related to that. I think that happens more than we know. It's a modern way of dealing with a bad life.

'I'm just glad,' Eddie told Cameron Crowe, 'that I became a songwriter.'

For the moment, though, Eddie didn't think the songs needed explaining. He just wanted someone to hear them, and as soon as possible.

That night, he worked patiently on the art work for the cassette sleeve. He titled the package 'Mamasan', and the next morning he mailed it to the contact address in Seattle that Jack Irons had given him and waited for a phone call.

Together, these three songs constituted what Eddie would later describe as a kind of 'mini-opera' (again, shades of the Who's Pete Townshend and both 'Quadropehenia' and 'Tommy'). They told a story, the full details of which would only emerge later. By then, 'Alive' had been adopted bythousands of America's disenfranchised young as a clarion call, a kind of life-affirming anthem, which is certainly something Eddie had never intended it to be.

'The story of the song is that a mother is with a father, and the father dies,' he told Cameron Crowe, obviously eager to clear this up. 'It's an intense thing because the son looks just like the father. The son grows up to *be* the father, the person that she lost. His father's dead, and now this confusion, his mother, his love, how does he love her, how does she love him? In fact, the mother, even though she marries somebody else, there's no one she's ever loved more than

Seattle Be The Day

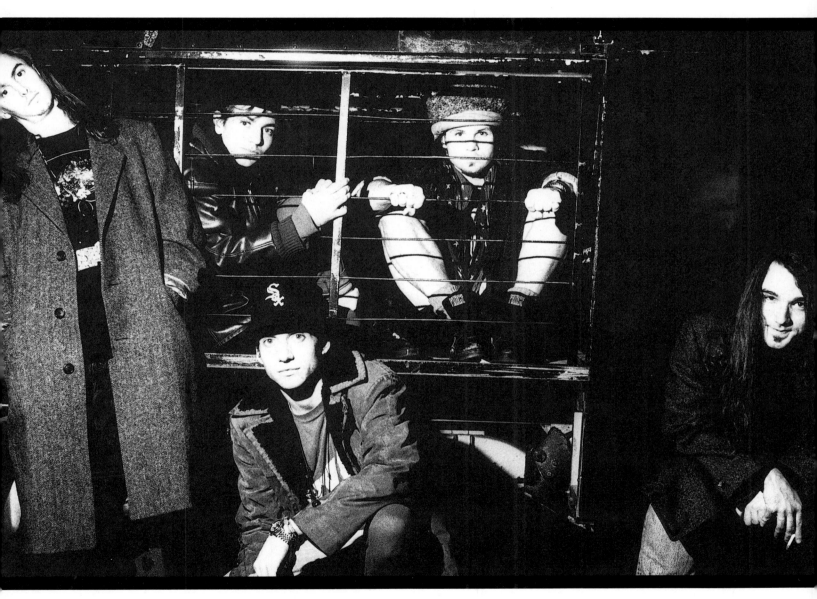

'**S**TONE,' he said, 'you better get over here.' You can only begin to imagine the excitement in Jeff Ament's voice when he called Stone Gossard the day he got Eddie Vedder's 'Mamasan' tape and played it through three times straight, hardly able to breathe by the end of the last playback. What Jeff was listening to was pretty close to being unbelievable.

He must have had the feeling that things were certainly never going to be the same again, that all the things that had so recently been going so wrong for him and Stone were somehow going to be put right, and that they had somehow found what they had been looking for.

Jeff had been in Seattle for nearly ten years by now, since quitting the University of Montana in his native Missoula, where he'd been studying art and indulging a passion for basketball. Disenchanted by what he found offensive, beery and sexist about the jock mentality he encountered at college, Jeff had started playing bass and formed a punk band called Deranged Diction.

He'd brought the group out to the Pacific Northwest in the early Eighties, and it had been one long struggle to get things going. He'd been in town a couple of months with Deranged Diction when he first met Stone, the son of a Seattle lawyer. At the time, Stone, who had been brought up on a pretty uninhibited musical diet of glam rock and heavy metal, was playing in The Ducky Boys, a band he had formed at high school with his friend Steve Turner.

In the usual incestuous way of these things, Turner was simultaneously gigging with another band, The Limp Richards, the side project of another local guitarist, Mark Arm. Arm, who already had a reputation for not giving much of a fuck about anything that might be mistaken for a professional attitude to music, was also involved with a couple of other Seattle bands, including Mr Epp And The Calculations and The Thrown-Ups, with whom Turner also occasionally appeared.

Unlike Arm and Turner, Jeff and Stone were both ambitious, which is something

Mudhoney with Mark Arm on far right, the first Sub-Pop band to break in the UK

Stone Gossard, from the days of the Ducky Boys a pivotal character in the often incestuous evolution of Pearl Jam

they liked about each other in a community of musicians whose aims were often only loosely defined. But so far into both their respective careers, none of the groups they'd been in had been remotely successful and although they would shortly achieve a vaguely legendary status in the emerging mythology of the Seattle scene, they'd never even got within whistling distance of a record deal.

By the end of 1982, in fact, The Ducky Boys had broken up. When they split, Turner joined Arm in Mr Epp and also gigged with another outfit called Spluii Numa. Finally, Spluii Numa and Mr Epp combined, with Turner and Arm enlisting Ament from the disintegrating Deranged Diction and a new drummer, Alex Vincent. The new band was called Green River who were named after a local Seattle landmark and a 1969 Creedence Clearwater Revival album.

Mother Love Bone, with glam-rocker Andrew Wood in shades

Green River made their vinyl debut on 'Deep Six', a compilation album which also featured The Melvins and Soundgarden, that appeared in the summer of 1985 on Seattle's C/Z Records, the label that was subsequently responsible for the 'Teriyaki Asthma Vol 1', a compilation album that featured one of the earliest recorded appearances of Nirvana.

Stone, who'd been left on the sidelines following the collapse of The Ducky Boys, was called in to Green River not long after the release of 'Deep Six'. He joined as co-guitarist with Steve Turner, allowing Mark Arm to concentrate on vocals. Gossard was a member in time to record 'Come On Down', a five-track 12 inch EP, released by the influential independent label Homestead in the summer of 1985, alongside 'Dinosaur', the debut LP by Dinosaur Jr.

TENSIONS

Not long after the EP's release, Steve Turner quit the band and was replaced on guitar by Bruce Fairweather, who'd played in Deranged Diction with Jeff. The new line-up recorded another five-track EP, 'Dry As A Bone', in the summer of 1986. It was a year before it came out, however, by which time Green River were on Sub Pop, the label that was shortly to become synonymous with grunge, a churning hybrid of slowed-down punk and Seventies heavy metal that defined the Seattle sound of the late-Eighties, and which subsequently became an international buzzword with the worldwide success of Nirvana's 1991 LP, 'Nevermind'.

'Green River destroyed the morals of a generation,' according to Bruce Pavitt, who founded Sub Pop with Jonathan Poneman, the manager of Soundgarden, another of the new generation of Seattle bands. Looking at early press shots of Green River, you can see that Pavitt had a point. Ament and Gossard look like they've just auditioned for The New York Dolls, while Arm had an

enthusiasm for appearing on stage in a variety of frocks and petticoats. Whatever their sartorial shortcomings, Green River were enormously influential. The typically ferocious mix of Gossard and Fairweather's metallic riffing and Arm's rasping punk yelping on 'Dry As A Bone' is widely regarded as the blueprint for grunge. It was followed in June 1988 by an eight-track mini-LP, 'Rehab Doll', which included a raucous cover of David Bowie's 'Queen Bitch' and a song called 'Together We'll Never', which had been released earlier as a single on the ICP label.

By now the tensions in the band were simmering. Gossard and Fairweather's metal leanings were becoming too much for Arm, who wanted a much rawer, punk sound. Arm was by now also in almost daily conflict with Jeff Ament. Arm shared the suspicion of major labels that would come to characterise the more intransigent Seattle bands while Jeff had no reservations about courting the big record companies. Things came to a spectacular pitch between the two in 1987, at a Halloween gig in Los Angeles, where Green River had been booked as support to Jane's Addiction.

Arm was livid when he discovered that Jeff had taken the names of a lot of the band's friends off the guest list for that night's show and replaced them with the names of major label A&R people he was trying to get interested in Green River. Arm was even more furious when most of the A&R men Jeff had invited to the gig didn't even bother to turn up. As far as Arm was concerned, Ament had betrayed the essential principles of independence he thought Green River should stand for.

After an angry row he walked out on the group. Reunited with the disaffected Steve Turner, the pair formed Mudhoney, whose quintessential grunge anthem, 'Touch Me,

I'm Sick', released as a single in August 1988, and the subsequent 'Superfuzz Bigmuff' mini-album, were the first Sub Pop records to make an impression in the United Kingdom.

The row that led to him quitting Green River left Arm full of resentment at what he saw as Ament's naked ambition. After the split, he kept up a long-running campaign of sniping criticism of his former band member in which he enlisted the vocal support of Nirvana's Kurt Cobain, who claimed to similarly abhor Ament's selling out to the forces of commercialism. This was seen as a bit rich

coming from someone who'd signed to the massive Geffen organisation, but by then what had started as a vague animosity toward Ament, whom Cobain barely knew, had turned into a full-scale vendetta against Pearl Jam.

When Arm marched out on Green River, the band was effectively over. Vincent quit the music business completely. Ament, Gossard and Fairbrother recruited drummer Greg Gilmour, veteran of Seattle outfits like Ten Minute Warning, while Arm was replaced by the flamboyant Andrew Wood, who'd previously fronted the ill-starred Malfunkshun, one of the bands who'd also appeared on 'Deep Six'.

Wood, who liked to be addressed by everyone as L'Andrew, was an aspiring glam idol. He liked to paint his face white and was prone to dress in silver suits and motorcycle boots that made him look like a cross between Ziggy Stardust and a Hell's Angel. On stage, his appearance was said to be even more outlandish. 'He was a total rock star,' Jonathan Poneman later remarked, 'even though he was the only person who thought so.'

DISILLUSION

Wood was a brilliantly charismatic frontman and singer, but he had one major problem: an addiction to heroin that would prove eventually disastrous for himself and his new band, who were called Lords Of The Wasteland for a while, before being re-named Mother Love Bone, after a line from 'Capricorn Sister', one of the first songs Wood had written with Stone.

Formed toward the end of 1987 in the immediate aftermath of the acrimonious Green River split, it was two years before Mother Love Bone released their first record, the five track 'Shine' EP, which was issued on the band's own Stardog label and distrib-uted by PolyGram, with whom they would eventually sign a long-term deal.

It looked finally like Stone and Jeff were at last heading for the big time that they'd always yearned for and which had so far eluded them. By the early autumn of 1989, they'd completed their debut album, the often stunning 'Apple'. Advance copies of the LP were circulated to unanimously enthusiastic reactions, but on Friday, March 16, 1990, four weeks before its official release date, that grim old babe called tragedy knocked at their door. Wood, who'd spent the last couple of months of 1989 going through a detox programme at the Valley General Hospital Alcohol & Drug Recovery Centre, just outside Seattle, and was now supposedly clean, was found

unconscious in his apartment by his girl-friend Xana LaFuente. Wood was rushed to the Harborview Medical Centre where he never regained consciousness. Three days into what the doctors described as being an irreversible coma, his family gave permis-sion for the life-support system that had been keeping him alive to be switched off. His parents, brothers, Xana LaFuente and the remaining members of Mother Love

released in July, but the surviving Mother Love Bone members were dropped by PolyGram and the band quickly split.

Two years of hard work had been buried along with Wood, and this might have been the final disappointment for Gossard and Ament. But Stone was determined to carry on somehow. After a period of mourning, he started working on new material, shifting from the ornate atmospherics of MLB

Soundgarden's Chris Cornell, organiser of the Temple Of The Dog tribute to Andrew Wood

Bone were present. A tape of Queen's 'A Night At The Opera' played in the back-ground, and Andrew Wood was dead. A post-mortem established the cause of death as a heroin overdose.

Wood's death had a numbing effect on the whole Seattle scene; Mother Love Bone themselves were devastated. Not only had they lost a close friend, everything they'd worked for had been destroyed. 'Apple' was

towards something harder and less trippy. As his new music started taking shape, he began looking for musicians. His first recruit was a spunky 24 year old Seattle guitarist named Mike McCready, whom he had known vaguely since high school.

McCready had grown up listening to his parent's Hendrix and Santana albums, though by the time he bought his first guitar, a Mateo Les Paul copy, at the age of 11, he

Green River with (left to right) Jeff Ament, Mark Arm, Stone Gossard, Steve Turner and Alex Vincent

was besotted with Kiss and Aerosmith. In the eighth grade of high school, he formed a band, Warrior, which in turn became known as Shadow. McCready was now also into UK metal bands like Def Leppard, Iron Maiden and Thin Lizzy. Other major influences on the young McCready were Eddie Van Halen and Ozzy Osbourne's guitarist Randy Rhoads, who was tragically killed in a flying accident in 1982.

McCready left high school in 1987, and Shadow moved to Los Angeles looking for a record deal. They spent 13 months there, hustling for gigs and getting nowhere fast. It was a sobering, cheerless time.

'We played to a couple of bartenders down there,' McCready would subsequently recall. 'But even though it was a bad scene, it was a good experience. Basically, we weren't that great a band, and we didn't realise it until we got down there. I guess we lost our focus. I got really bummed out and came back to Seattle.'

Six months later, Shadow folded. It was 1988 and McCready was so disillusioned

and depressed that he virtually gave up music. He enrolled at a local college, cut his hair and got a job in a video store. He would later credit a friend named Russ Riedner with reviving his interest in music. He began to rebuild his career cautiously, jamming with friends, making no big deal at first of his rekindled enthusiasm for playing. Soon he formed Love Chile, a psychedelic blues band, with whom he was playing in Seattle when he got a completely unexpected call from Stone Gossard.

They had rarely been in contact since high school, but as soon as they started playing together something clicked in a big way. Stone's strong sense of rhythm and melody and McCready's incendiary lead style complemented each other with a dynamic perfection that surprised them both.

'Whatever you're playing, 'Cready comes in and lights the fuse,' Gossard remarked later, recalling their early sparring sessions.

Ament, meanwhile, was depressed and drifting, gigging around Seattle with a bar band called The War Babies and picking up a

few extra bucks with a loose jamming outfit, Luv Company. Gossard got in touch with him and explained his plans for the new group he was putting together. Ament was persuaded to join and he and McCready started jamming regularly in the attic of Stone's parents house, where Green River and Mother Love Bone had also organised their first rehearsals.

Around September 1990, they began recording demos. The material they laid down was based mostly on Stone's tunes, riffs and arrangements. One of the tracks that most excited them was a song that Stone had actually started writing in Mother Love Bone. They worked it up now and gave it a title. They called it 'Dollar Short' and it became the centrepiece of the demo that found its way to Eddie Vedder in San Diego and inspired him to write 'Alive'. As soon as Gossard and McCready heard the tape that had excited Ament, they knew that they had their man.

They told Jeff to call Eddie in San Diego and invite him up to Seattle.

Say Hello 2 Heaven

Ready for Take off

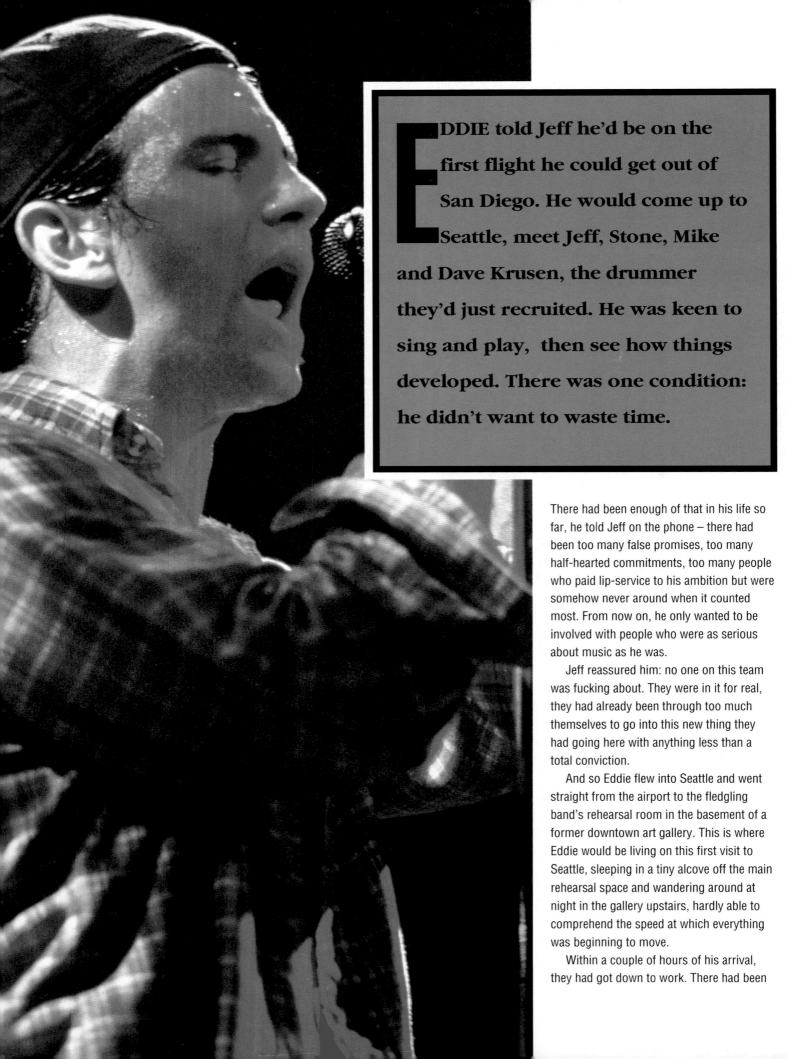

EDDIE told Jeff he'd be on the first flight he could get out of San Diego. He would come up to Seattle, meet Jeff, Stone, Mike and Dave Krusen, the drummer they'd just recruited. He was keen to sing and play, then see how things developed. There was one condition: he didn't want to waste time.

There had been enough of that in his life so far, he told Jeff on the phone – there had been too many false promises, too many half-hearted commitments, too many people who paid lip-service to his ambition but were somehow never around when it counted most. From now on, he only wanted to be involved with people who were as serious about music as he was.

Jeff reassured him: no one on this team was fucking about. They were in it for real, they had already been through too much themselves to go into this new thing they had going here with anything less than a total conviction.

And so Eddie flew into Seattle and went straight from the airport to the fledgling band's rehearsal room in the basement of a former downtown art gallery. This is where Eddie would be living on this first visit to Seattle, sleeping in a tiny alcove off the main rehearsal space and wandering around at night in the gallery upstairs, hardly able to comprehend the speed at which everything was beginning to move.

Within a couple of hours of his arrival, they had got down to work. There had been no fuss, barely time for introductions. Everyone sensed something major taking shape here and no one, caught up in a fierce enthusiasm, wanted to waste time.

Eddie was in his element, what was going on was a kind of heaven for him.

'Those first few days we were together,' he later recalled, 'were just magical for all of us. As soon as we got together, we knew we could depend on each other. We had a band.'

The first song they played together was 'Alive'. Eddie, meanwhile, had arrived in town with another new song, 'Black'. They had a crack at that, and it seemed to come together almost immediately. This was the kind of creative environment Eddie had been looking for since he first got into the idea of making music. He couldn't believe what was happening. Neither could the band, as Eddie kept coming up with more and more songs. Soon they were working on 'Why Go' and 'Oceans'.

By the end of that first week, they knew they were a band. All they needed was a name. Stuck for inspiration on this particular front, they ended up calling the band after a basketball player, Mookie Blaylock, who was then guard for the New Jersey Nets. 'That first week when we were much too busy working on music to think of anything like a band name,' Eddie explained, 'his basketball card ended up in our tape, so we kind of took him on right there.'

On the sixth day they were together, the newly-christened Mookie Blaylock were ready for their first show, at a joint called The Off Ramp.

'We sucked,' Eddie subsequently admitted. 'The songs were all there, but I think, obviously, it was like a rehearsal in front of a lot of people.'

IN THE TEMPLE OF THE DOG

They knew by now, however, that they had more going for them than they had dared hope for. They were going to give this their best shot. Whatever they retrospectively thought were the shortcomings of their debut at The Off Ramp, they instinctively

knew that they'd tapped into something, that this hasty coalition that had come together in that week of intense rehearsal was a unit they could build upon and develop into something unique, something very special and permanent.

There was one piece of unfinished business to be taken care of, however, before they could give their full attention to their own new direction. One member of the Seattle musical community who'd been most affected by Andrew Wood's death was Chris Cornell, the singer with Soundgarden, who by now had become the first of the Sub Pop generation to be signed by a major American label, A&M, for whom they were already working the 'Badmotorfinger' album, which would take them into the US Top 10.

Cornell had once shared an apartment with Wood, and had always felt a close affinity with him. In the immediate aftermath of Wood's untimely death, Cornell had written two songs as a kind of tribute to his friend. 'Reach Down' and 'Say Hello 2 Heaven' were simply two of the best things Cornell had ever written, but he didn't at first know quite what to do with this material. He thought vaguely about making a solo album that would stand as a posthumous tribute to Wood and would simultaneously be an act of exorcism, a final laying to rest of Wood's glam rock ghost.

Still trying to work out the precise musical parameters of this peculiar requiem, Cornell eventually called Gossard and Ament and asked them to help him shape the songs he'd written in his hours of darkness and grief into something that would be a more

Grunge – punk energy and heavy dynamics

coherently legible musical epitaph.

Stone and Jeff were by then working with Mike McCready on what would become the legendary 'Stone Gossard Demos' tape. As soon as Cornell contacted them, however, they agreed to meet and discuss the project. The brought McCready along to the sessions Cornell had already booked. What had begun as some notion of a Cornell solo project – maybe just a single, possibly an EP – now turned into a full-blown album.

The one-off band they had inadvertently become called themselves Temple Of The Dog, after the line of a lyric to a Mother Love Bone song. The line-up for the recording consisted of Cornell, Stone, Jeff, Mike and Soundgarden drummer Matt Cameron, who'd played on the 'Stone Gossard Demos' tape. When Eddie Vedder hit town for the rehearsals that would lead to the formation of what would eventually become Pearl Jam, he was hauled in, too.

Vedder by all accounts was a huge Soundgarden fan, and in awe of Cornell. Nervous as he might have felt, Eddie ended up not only singing on the 'Temple Of The Dog' album, but also contributing a song to it. With new lyrics written by Cornell, 'Times Of Trouble' was a version of 'Footsteps', part of the 'mini-opera' trilogy Vedder had sent only a couple of weeks earlier to Jeff Ament on the 'Mamasan' tape.

STRAPPED TO THE ROCKET

'Temple Of The Dog' originally came out in May 1991, and for Stone and Jeff, it was the final amen to Andrew Wood, and the closing of a chapter in their careers that had once promised so much but which had ended in tears and death. They were more than ever ready to begin again.

The oddly-named Mookie Blaylock, as they were still uncomfortably called at the time, began gigging regularly in Seattle. It didn't seem to matter too much to them where they played, as long as there was something they could call a stage and something that looked like an audience. What mattered most to them all was the simple fact that they were *together*, that they were

Opposite, Eddie at New York's CBGB's, late '91. Above, left and right, Jeff Ament and Mike McCready

continuing to write. Even in what were still relatively early days, they had a collective sense that they were beginning to assemble a genuinely formidable repertoire of original material.

Stone, Jeff and Mike were by now pretty much veterans of this kind of gig circuit. They knew how to handle a crowd, were uninhibited in front of audiences. They threw rock 'n' roll shapes, were unselfconscious, grooving. Eddie, on the other hand, was still brooding, uncertain and nervous. People still remember those early shows in Seattle, and they talk about Eddie being so introverted and painfully shy he was almost unable to make eye contact with his audience.

This all changed in a big way when Mookie Blaylock went out on a tour of Canada with Alice In Chains. They were at some godforsaken dive called Harpo's in Victoria, British Columbia. It was the first time they'd appeared outside the nurturing environment of Seattle, where they'd been used to supportive, enthusiastic audiences. The crowd that night at Harpo's were mean, indifferent. There was something beery and ugly in the air, a kind of sullen hostility.

Midway through their set, Eddie decided

he'd had enough. He hadn't hauled his ass all the way up here to be treated with such pathetic, cross-eyed disrespect. He was going to make these people wake the fuck up and pay attention. If Eddie had anything to do with it, this drag-assed crowd was going to witness a performance they'd definitely never forget.

CIRCUS EVENT

No one later could remember what they were playing when Eddie made his move, but they could recall Eddie, in the middle of whatever song they were cranking out up there on the stage at Harpo's, starting to unscrew the 12-pound steel base of his microphone stand. There may, however, have been a few unsettled looks from the farting drongo hordes, the beer-swilling pot-bellied Canuck jocks and their sagging-buttocked girlfriends as Eddie slowly and deliberately continued his meticulous dismantling of his mike stand. Then, with a flourish that became legendary, Eddie, with the dangerous gleam in his eye that would characterise subsequent gigs, sent the heavy steel base whipping through the air, inches above the heads of the agape crowd. It flew fully 50 or 60 feet and hit the

back wall of the club with a sickening, teeth-rattling crash.

He had their fucking attention now.

'It was a big turning point for Eddie,' Jeff Ament would recall with a certain wry amusement.

From here on in until it became what Jeff would later describe as a 'circus event', Eddie's stage persona was outlandish, dangerous and breathtaking. Whatever there was on or near to the stage that he could climb, Eddie climbed, clambered and scaled. He climbed the stage scaffolding and lighting rigs, hauled himself to the top of speaker stacks and balconies.

Years before, Iggy Pop had literally walked all over his audience, stepping off stage onto a sea of upturned hands that supported his deranged strolls. Eddie took this bizarre ritual to new and even more unhinged extremes. What Eddie did was pretty much invent crowd surfing. The music would reach peaks of excitement that few audiences had previously witnessed, and Eddie, caught up in the wild colossal turmoil of the moment, would launch himself from the stage, diving into what at every gig was becoming an increasingly hysterical throng,

Of constant concern to Eddie Vedder is his relationship, on stage as well as off, with his fans

Jeff Ament relaxes, San Francisco 1992

and be passed, hand-over hand, head-over-head, from one end of whatever bar, club, or hall his band were playing. Night after night, he'd be returned to the stage, bitten, cut and bleeding, chunks pulled out of him, wide-eyed with the delirium he was more and more aware of creating, and over which he was able to exert less and less control.

'That climbing happened out of me saying: "Look, this is how extreme I feel about this situation. This is how fucking intense I'm taking this moment," ' Eddie told Cameron Crowe. 'You can't do that for long, because what they really want to see is, they want you to chop your fucking arm off, hold up your arm, wave it around spewing blood, and believe me, if you did that, the crowd would go fucking *ballistic*. You only get four good shows, and then you're just a torso and a head, trying to get one of your band mates to give you one last hurrah and chop your head off.'

Things would eventually get so out of control and expectations of his psychotic acrobatics would become so intense that Eddie would by force of circumstance have to revert to something approaching the more withdrawn and guarded performances that had characterised his first appearances with Mookie Blaylock. But for the moment it was an aspect of the still-young, still-growing band's live shows that attracted the attention of an increasingly slavering music business that had been alerted to the commercial potential of the so-called 'Seattle sound' by the unprecedented runaway success of Nirvana's 'Nevermind'.

From being regarded as just an obscure backwater, famous mostly for being the birthplace of Jimi Hendrix, Seattle by the beginning of the Nineties was an A&R man's dream. Pavitt and Poneman had started Sub Pop with the explicit aim of promoting local talent. Now Seattle was on the international

As the audience reaction at Pearl Jam concerts got wilder and wilder, only the brave or foolish tried to make their way to the front

agenda. There was a thriving creative scene there that the major labels thought they could exploit. Every label looking for musical credibility immediately sent their talent scouts and A&R sharks to the Northwest, cheque books in hand, to sign virtually everything that moved.

Mookie Blaylock had by now changed their name to Pearl Jam, a name suggested by Eddie, and inspired by his grandmother.

'Old Grandma Pearl was married to an Indian guy and they kind of shared cultures,' he explained. 'The ultimate example of that sharing would be the preserves she made using insane ingredients, like peyote. But she made it into something you could spread . . . a hallucinogenic preserve. You know, "Throw a little on your muffin and have a nice day, sweetheart."'

In the early autumn of 1991, they were offered a deal with Epic, part of the vast Sony Columbia empire. Almost before the

ink was dry on the contract, they had made the basic tracks for their debut album with Rick Parashar who had produced the 'Temple Of The Dog' album, which in a wryly touching gesture they would eventually call 'Ten', after Mookie Blaylock's team number.

The group were about to fly to England to mix the album at Ridge Farm Studios in Dorking with Tim Palmer when Dave Krusen suddenly announced that he had decided to quit the band.

'I was going through some personal problems,' he explained later. 'Me and my girlfriend had a baby the day after we went in to record the album. It was a lot of pressure on me and I didn't handle it very well. I kinda drank too much. It got to the point where I needed to go into treatment.'

The rest of the band flew to England. Krusen went into rehab in an attempt to clean himself up and also to reconcile his differences with his girlfriend. He managed

to kick his drink habit, but there was no patching things up with his girlfriend. She left him soon after he came out of detox. He was sober, but he no longer had a girlfriend and he no longer had a band. Pearl Jam, meanwhile, were looking for a replacement.

They first of all recruited Matt Chamberlain, who'd previously been playing with Eddie Brickell And The New Bohemians. But Chamberlain couldn't stand the pace, however, and when he was offered what he thought would be more regular work as a member of the *Saturday Night Live* house band, he quit.

As a parting gesture, he suggested as his replacement a drummer he knew in Texas, Dave Abruzzese. Born in Stamford, Connecticut, Abruzzese attended grade school in East Harford and Manchester before moving south to North Carolina with his family. A year later, the Abruzzeses moved to Houston. He'd been living there for nearly 12 years and was playing in a funk band called Dr Tongue and co-hosting a radio show, *Music We Like*, when Cameron called him and told him that he knew a bunch of guys in Seattle who'd just recorded an album that was due out soon, with a tour to follow, who were looking for a drummer.

Abruzzese wasn't much interested at first, but Chamberlain persuaded him to fly up to Seattle to give it some kind of try. A week of rehearsals and a couple of shows later, Dave was a more than willing recruit. His initial reservations had been broken down by the power of the music Pearl Jam were playing, and he wanted to be part of it. As a physical example of his serious commitment to the band, he even had the stick-figure Pearl Jam logo that Jeff Ament had designed tattooed on his shoulder.

With their debut album ready for release, Pearl Jam, with Abruzzese installed in the drum seat, began the heavy touring schedule that would keep them on the road for over a year. They played wherever and whenever they could, all over America, in whatever backwater that would have them. In the process, they attracted a massive fan base, possibly larger and more enthusiastic than they ever realised at the time.

By the end of the year, with 'Ten' for the moment still selling only modestly, they went out on a kind of package tour with Smashing Pumpkins and The Red Hot Chili Peppers. As the tour progressed, they were beginning to get more hysterical reactions than the headliners and 'Ten' started selling harder and faster and was hurtling towards the American Top 10. On New Year's Eve, they played San Francisco's Cow Palace, opening for the Chili Peppers and Nirvana. There were frightening scenes of mass adulation.

This kind of audience response was what they'd been working towards, of course. Some of their Seattle peers were appalled at what they thought was a blatant willingness to embrace commercial success while they continued to wallow in their own insufferable fuck-you truculence when it came to dealing with major labels. But Pearl Jam had never wanted to be anything less than successful commercially, not because they were merely interested in the material gain of rock'n'roll stardom, but because they truly believed that the music they were playing deserved to be heard by the widest possible audience. Even so, with the album 'Ten' selling more and more thousands of copies every week, the speed at which things were going plainly staggered them.

As Cameron Crowe memorably observed, Pearl Jam had been built basically for a slow build. Now they found themselves strapped to the rocket.

They were preparing for take-off, in a way they could never really have imagined.

Within another few months, they'd be one of the biggest bands in America, and then the world.

Seattle to San Francisco, 1992

★★★★★★★★★★★★★★★★★★

Counting To Ten

Rockin' the Vote

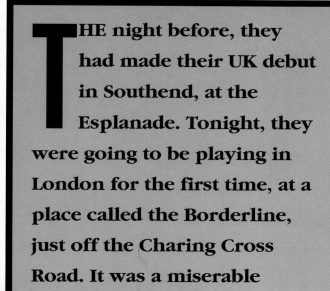

The Borderline was a club in the basement of an ersatz Mexican restaurant called Break For The Border. Record companies used it a lot for showcase gigs – R.E.M. had played here, for instance, as Bingo Hand Job, when they were promoting 'Out Of Time' with a series of appearances throughout Europe at small clubs. For a band like R.E.M., playing somewhere as small as the Borderline was a cool idea, an opportunity for their fans to see them in an intimate environment. The only problem was that the fans, the people who would have most enjoyed this gesture, were mostly excluded from the gig. Tickets for the two shows R.E.M. played, for instance, were incredibly scarce. Most of them had been snapped up by their record company and distributed within the music business – to journalists, people from TV and radio, agents, bookers, promoters, friends of friends. The same thing happened when Pearl Jam played the Borderline. Outside the club that night, there was a bedraggled, disgruntled crowd, bristling with resentment. It was more ammunition for their critics, of course. Nirvana, they claimed, had never pulled a stunt like this, playing for a privileged minority. It was just Pearl Jam being rock stars, entertaining a dubious music biz elite.

It was by now obvious that Pearl Jam were going to be the kind of band who would excite passionately contradictory opinions. For the faithfully converted, of which I was emphatically one after nearly a month of listening with increasing awe to an advance tape of 'Ten', they were already the band of the moment, if not the year. The heretical take on them was that they were

THE night before, they had made their UK debut in Southend, at the Esplanade. Tonight, they were going to be playing in London for the first time, at a place called the Borderline, just off the Charing Cross Road. It was a miserable February night, sleet in the air, very cold.

somehow contrived, Epic's corporate response to Guns N' Roses and Nirvana, Geffen's twin money-spinners.

This was patent nonsense, of the highest order. As *Melody Maker*'s David Stubbs had pointed out in his review of 'Alive' when it was released as a single, Pearl Jam were here because they were driven, almost obsessed, by a need to communicate, tell us something about our lives and what happens to us when we are caught in the crossfire of ferocious emotional extremes. Pearl Jam had something to say: it was often brutal and disquieting and there were no easy truths or reassurances. But they were determined to make you *listen* and they sounded like they might be prepared to die in the attempt. Pearl Jam were out there, man, in the same way that Jane's Addiction, say, or American Music Club or Thin White Rope were out there.

Thinking about it further, as the Borderline filled up that night, it seemed to me that while Pearl Jam were undoubtedly destined to attract vast chunks of their respective audiences, the Guns/Nirvana comparison was eventually too stifling. For sure, there were aspects of 'Ten' – the incendiary guitar firestorms whipped up by Gossard and McCready, the general in-yer-face attitude they put out – that made you think of the Geffen money bears. But listening to this remarkable record, I could also hear echoes of Neil Young & Crazy Horse, of R.E.M., of The Replacements and – unlikely, I know – of Tim Buckley. These were people who worshipped in the broad church of American music.

They were obviously no one man show, but what provided them with such a unique and compelling focus was the presence of Eddie Vedder.

'Ten' opened up with a weird snatch of ambient voodoo rhythm twitches before the guitars blasted into overdrive, but the first thing you *really* heard was Eddie's voice. It was like a helicopter rotor blade, a gash in the air.

'Once . . . upon a time . . . I could . . . CONTROL MYSELF!' he roared. And you

London's Borderline club was the venue for the band's media breakthrough in Great Britain

knew you were in some kind of psychic bad-lands where all bets were off and life was the thing you were living, but maybe for not much longer. 'Got a bomb in my temple that's gonna explode,' Eddie sang over the guitar meltdown. 'Got a 16 gauge buried under my clothes . . . '

This was Eddie as Travis Bickle, the avenging angel of Martin Scorsese's *Taxi Driver*, the deranged Vietnam vet of Buckley's 'Nighthawkin', Crispen Glover very creepy in *River's Edge*, and Christian Slater dusting the local high school population in *Heathers*. To some extent, this was the same territory that The Replacement's Paul Westerberg had staked out as his own as early as 'Sorry, Ma, Forgot To Take Out The Trash' and further refined to a burnished point of sullenly beautiful perfection on 'All Shook Down'.

Eddie's songscapes were populated by the terminally fucked-up - losers, loners, the deranged and the damned, derelict children of trailer parks and housing tracts. Even Westerberg, that laureate of American nihilism, had rarely written with such urgency about the victims of America. 'Why Go', for instance, was a dark, harrowing description of a young girl's detention in a mental institution. 'She's been diagnosed by some stupid fuck,' Eddie raged. It was a basic point – the world is much madder than anyone in it – but it was vividly expressed and played with a ghastly power.

The sheer force of these songs pinned your arse to the carpet and made you squirm. The most coruscating of them was probably the six minute 'Jeremy'. It had been inspired by a story in a Texan newspaper, about a kid who was bullied and abused so

Jeff Ament at the Borderline

The sheer energy of an Eddie Vedder performance is captured in this phased image at the Borderline show

badly at school that one day in English class he simply blew his brains out. Just the guitar crescendos made it compulsory listening, but Eddie's staggering vocal performance took it deeper into the void than you might willingly have wished to go.

Pearl Jam didn't want to leave you in an alley, bleeding. 'Jeremy' was as bleak as the album got. Elsewhere, there were moments of blinding redemptive light. 'I know some day you'll have a beautiful life,' Vedder sang with enormous heartfelt compassion on the ominously-titled 'Black'. And it was as heart-breaking as the 'please be happy, baby' refrain from American Music Club's 'Western Skies'. 'Ocean', meanwhile, was like something off the first side of 'Starsailor', Tim Buckley's visionary master-piece, all rolling tympani, grazed shards of guitars and Vedder's voice coasting a

tremendous octave range.

'Garden' and the climactic 'Release' were the kind of songs destined even then to become stadium anthems and put up the sales of Zippos at a stroke. I was normally invulnerable to this sort of misty-eyed romanticism, but Pearl Jam made it work with a rare and unforgettable intensity. And the guitars were just great: growling like Young and Crazy Horse on the slowburning 'Garden', gleaming like stroked lightning on 'Release'. Vedder's voice was at its most operatic here. But it wasn't bombastic like Bono, it was perfectly cool. 'Pavarotti sings Stipe,' said a friend.

And then we were back to the beginning, the album fading with an extended reprise of the *gris-gris* hum that had introduced it.

'Ten', it seemed to me then and still seems to me now, was the sound of rock the

way she was meant to be rolled.

They came on to a wall of noise. But it wasn't applause or cheering from the faithful throng at the front of the low, cramped stage. It was the people at the back of the Borderline, trying to order food, and people at the bar ordering drinks and chattering, self-important and garrulous, and oblivious to the fact that something was starting to happpen. No wonder the fans outside were furious. This was sheer ignorance beyond understanding.

LOVE THIS BAND

On stage, Pearl Jam started with a song called 'Wash', and it seemed tentative, just the bare stirrings of something, the band's engine warming up. They seemed to be just flexing their muscles, getting a feel for the place, surprisingly nonchalant in a variety of hats, boots, baggy shorts, singlets and hair. The crowd at the bar were still chattering. Then Pearl Jam went into 'Once'. And about five minutes later, when the dust had finally settled, no one was talking. Everyone's attention was locked on the stage. Here and there, heads were shaking in various degrees of stunned disbelief. What the fuck had just happened here?

I was transfixed, bug-eyed with sheer astonishment.

'Even Flow' and 'Alive' followed. They were basically tearing through the soon-come 'Ten' like someone had told them this into the audience.

Time seemed to stretch. I kept flashing back nearly ten years, to R.E.M.'s British debut at Dingwall's, a club in north London, not much bigger than the Borderline. It was a freezing November night, a Saturday, there were maybe 50 or 60 people in the audience, and none of us who were there will ever forget it, the band coming on like a cross – believe it! – between The Sex Pistols and The Byrds, and Michael Stipe in some kind of cardigan or jumper he'd turned inside out, and was wearing back to front or something, that made it look like he was in a straitjacket.

alter your perception of the power of music. If music is a big part of your life, it's the same difference. It's Big and Important, and both your head and your heart want each other to sort it out.

'But watching Vedder sing those songs, the way his eyeballs roll back into his skull, his lips stretched across his face in a rictus grin, his teeth clenched like they're going to shatter . . . how can he feel such hurt and hate, and still make such soulful, uplifting music? There's the mystery. That's Pearl Jam. Love this band.'

Within a couple of days, Andrew Mueller

A genuine concern for his fellow humans permeates much of Vedder's lyrics

Pearl Jam in Oslo, 1992

was the last gig they'd ever play. I remember Eddie talking about his parents being dead, and you began to wonder whether he was telling us that he'd killed them. During 'Black', the intensity of their performance was almost suffocating, Eddie's anguish coming off the stage in waves. 'Why Go' came and went, Eddie rolling on the floor, being grabbed at, beyond comprehension in his ecstatic state, eyes blazing like spotlights, arms outstretched as if he was someone waiting to be crucified, and then falling

Stipe held my attention then as Eddie Vedder held it now. I couldn't take my eyes off Stipe at Dingwall's, I couldn't take my eyes off Eddie here. He was a hypnotic and totally compelling presence.

Neil Perry, reviewing the Borderline gig for *Melody Maker*, captured what a lot of us must have been thinking that night.

'It can be mind-boggling,' he wrote, 'to try to put into words how you suddenly feel about a band who you know are going to have a radical effect on your life, or at least

was on his way to Oslo to interview Pearl Jam for *Melody Maker* and what turned out to be their first cover story anywhere. Mueller had missed the Borderline show, and was flabbergasted by the reaction the band provoked.

'I've never seen anything like this,' he reported. 'Saturday night in Oslo's Club Alaska, and your correspondent stands uneasily amid scenes suggesting rush hour at the New York Stock Exchange as choreographed by Caligula. The place is crammed, a mighty scrum of noise and chaos.

Whichever way you turn, weave, duck or run for cover, fists are being exchanged as enthusiastically as various body fluids, wild-eyed faces smeared with blood and/or lip-stick lurch fleetingly before you, glasses full of four-quid-a-pint lager are being lobbed about with random drunken abandon and, in front of the stage, a heaving, sweating moshpit swirls and churns under a continual hail of increasingly-acrobatic stagedivers. Digging myself into a nervous bridgehead behind a table at the back of the dancefloor, I've got a split toenail, a burnt hand, a rising

set I've witnessed, but they're that kind of band. See, as 'Porch' had rumbled on to a beautiful, messy end, Eddie had coiled up his microphone lead and thrown the mike, grappling-hook-like, up through a hole in the ventilation rig 12 or so feet above the stage. Using the cord as a leg-up, he climbs up into one of the man-sized horizontal holes and adjusts himself to face the audience. He keeps singing.

'The audience aren't this good in Seattle,' he bellows, to an ecstatic crowd reaction, and engineers himself headfirst out of his perch to cling, Spiderman-style, to the right

basketballers go sky-diving. Pearl Jam exit. The hysteria is palpable. It's one of the best half-dozen gigs I've ever seen.'

And there was more to come, as the weathermen are prone to say.

By the last week in February, Pearl Jam were back in the UK for gigs in Manchester, Newcastle, Glasgow, Nottingham, Birmingham, Bradford and, on February 28, a Friday no one who was there will find it easy to forget, they played the final date of their first British tour at the University of London Union.

Even before the group had played a note,

The Scandanavian tour, 1992

Mike McCready with Rolling Stones t-shirt

swell above the right ear, and *I'm* trying to keep out of trouble.

'And I'm thinking, Christ, it's gonna be hell in here when the band start playing . . .'

Mueller was right, and not for the first time. What followed was pretty infernal, heart-stopping, and unforgettable.

And this, according to Andrew's highly colourful account, is how it ended.

'Pearl Jam return for the first of umpteen encores. A game move, attempting to top about the most breathtaking finale to a live

angle between the wall and the ceiling. What follows seems to happen in slow-mo. Eddie spreads his arms wide, launches himself with his feet, and drops into the pit. He doesn't miss a beat . . . The carnage in front of the stage has, by now, reached a point well beyond metaphorical approximation.

'The encores keep coming, getting less coherent with each song and involving ever more members of the local support act. Jeff, for reasons best known to himself, is doing a go-go routine on top of his amp. Plastic

the area in front of the stage was like a war zone, bodies flying into a fiercely moshing crowd. When the band finally appeared, it must have seemed to Eddie Vedder that everything had got completely out of hand, all sense of control had been abandoned. He was suffering that night from a painfully sore throat, and his voice was almost gone. It can't have been easy for him to keep going, but he did. What started to annoy the fuck out of him, however, was the complete mindlessness of the stage diving, the feet-

Jeff and Eddie at Lollapalooza II in the Summer of '92

first reckless plunges from the stage onto the suffering broken heads of the roiling hysterical crowd at the front of the stage. People were getting hurt down there, and Eddie wasn't amused. This wasn't MTV, this wasn't the choreographed concert video for 'Alive'. This was happening for real, and it was getting obviously dangerous.
The crush in front of him was getting worse, the mob was getting wilder, more demented. Eddie kept stopping the show to berate the more insane stagedivers, his patience sorely tested by their thoughtlessness.
'You guys probably think you look like Jesus Christ,' he finally announced as another wave of manic stagedivers took off into the audience, arms outstretched. 'But, man, when I see you fucking things up like this, I just want to crucify you.'
And there was real anger in this, a genuine impatience. And it seemed to bug him. Even as the set continued, you sensed that he was

struggling with some kind of rage that he couldn't get out of his system. He was caught in a mess of contradictions. He had been criticising people for what? Imitating him, really, wanting to do something they'd seen *him* do, thinking it was cool.
And it seemed to occur to Eddie, thinking about it as the band roared on, that maybe he should somehow demonstrate to these people that this senseless diving, feet-first into a frightened crowd, was worth nothing, a demonstration of sheer uselessness, unless there was a real sense of danger involved. All that these people who had so obviously annoyed him were doing was hauling their fat arses onto the stage and flinging themselves onto innocent battered heads. Fuck that! He'd show them what it was really all about.
There was a windowsill or ledge of some kind running around the entire interior perimeter of the hall, maybe 20 feet above

us. Eddie got up there somehow, and started edging along it down the right hand side of the hall towards the balcony at the far end. It couldn't have been more than a couple of inches wide, so he used the curtains, heavy drapes hanging from rods higher still above him, swinging Tarzan-style along the ledge. He got to the balcony, found a way across to the other side of the hall. Then, swinging from curtain to curtain, he made his way along that ledge, back towards the stage. The band played on, wondering like everyone else what he was going to do next.
It was frightening, but exhilarating. You wanted him to stop, get down. This was the sensible parental option. An even bigger part of you, however, wanted him to take it as far as he was prepared to go, which seemed to be all the way, nothing less.
Which is where he took it, of course.
Twenty feet up, maybe more, he looked down. Who knows what he was thinking then. The band were riffing into something crazy, you couldn't catch your breath. There was a moment when it looked like Eddie was going to fall. The crowd gasped, as one, a vast inhalation, sucking what was left of the air in here into scorched exhausted lungs. We turned again to look at Eddie, up there, above us.
And then, he was falling . . . falling . . . falling . . . falling, arms outstretched, hair streaming behind him, a sky diver. And, falling, he seemed to fall for ever. The crowd caught him, of course. They almost buckled beneath his weight, but – yeah! – it was a great catch.
And then Eddie was back on the stage, grinning like a demon, everyone cheering. And you wondered if he'd made any point at all and where this would all end.
By now, 'Ten' was in the *Billboard* Top 10 and America was clamouring for more of Pearl Jam. They returned to the States in March, to record a stunning session for MTV's *Unplugged*. This was usually a showcase for a lot of venerable old codgers to present their back catalogue in an acoustic setting. The programmes were meant to be informal, a chance for viewers to admire the

Jubilant fans despite the cancellation of the Gas Works Park gig

consummate craftsmanship of rock's elder statesmen in a comfortable and intimate atmosphere. Mostly, the shows were merely dull, worthy to the point of tedium, self-regarding in the extreme. Pearl Jam's appearance was, however, a revelation. Even without their usual banks of amplification, they were electrifying.

That summer *MM*'s Stud Brothers flew out Seattle to meet Eddie Vedder and Pearl Jam. They were meant to be reporting on a free concert the band had organised as a kind of homecoming after all those months on the road. When the idea of the concert first came up, they imagined there'd be an audience of maybe 5000, tops. They had no idea how big they were getting. What they were looking at as the date for the show approached was a mini-Woodstock. People were heading to Seattle from all over America. There was wild talk of 30-40,000 of them turning up. This was a week after the LA riots, which sparked off demonstrations in a lot of US cities, including Seattle. The city's mayor and police department freaked. By the time the Studs hit town, the concert was off.

DETERMINATION

Eddie was furious, but undefeated. They might have stopped him this time, but he had other battles to fight, a bigger war to win. He was going to take on the Northwest

Eddie with Gas Works in the background

lumber barons who were plundering the forests, the Pro-Life anti-abortionists, the oil companies. He was involved in Rock The Vote, helping mobilise support for Bill Clinton's tilt at the White House. There were a hundred righteous causes he was prepared to commit himself to. The Stud Brothers were genuinely struck by his determination to leave his mark on the world, hit a lick for freedom, and his conviction that with energy and compassion and organisation the world might somehow be redeemed from the dire clutches of the thin-lipped multinational hit men whose only ambition it seemed to Eddie was the total destruction of the planet and everything on it. And what annoyed him almost as much was the ineffectuality of America's liberal and left wing coalitions in dealing with the threat to the environment – and to basic civil liberties – being posed by these people.

'The conservatives are well organised,' he said. 'They sit at home watching their church television channels, they have their letter-writing campaigns and they have a highly developed network going. They are using democracy in a supremely active way. The left-wing are more passive. They believe no one's gonna take their reproductive rights away, or stop them avoiding a pregnancy if they can't afford it. But the liberal left can't afford to think like that any more because these sixty-year-old fuckers are organising Pro-Life letter campaigns. Shit, they're sixty-year-olds. It's an issue that doesn't concern them any more. But they're still doing it. The left has a lot to learn from those guys. They need to get organised.'

The afternoon of the cancelled concert, Eddie went down Gas Works Park, site of the aborted show, where a large crowd had gathered. Eddie walked among them, signing autographs, shaking hands, apologising for having to cancel the show some of them had travelled hundreds of miles to see.

'Watching him,' the Studs wrote, 'thin, long-haired, followed by fresh-faced youths, you could be forgiven for thinking you were in the presence of a nightmarish, all-singing, all-dancing hybrid of John The Baptist and Robert Kennedy.'

You read the Studs' eventual account of their two or three days with Eddie in Seattle and came away with an impression of Eddie

The 'Jam in front of the Gas Works

as a slacker messiah, the Bono of grunge. Not that he wanted to be seen like this.

'I don't want to be a leader, I don't want to be a politician,' he told a not totally convinced Studs. 'But if people call on me, I'll be there.'

If they ever read what Eddie had to say to *Kerrang* magazine around the same time, the Studs would have been even more alarmed at Eddie's emerging sense of duty and indeed mission.

'I need honesty, I need truth, and I need hope – I need it! That's what music means to me. The first record came out the way it did, with its lyrical honesty, probably because I was so naive, but with the next one I'll be educated to strengthen my view.

'I knew I had to enjoy the struggle getting here, but now I can help people,' he told writer Liz Evans. 'I'm probably concerned with too many issues, animal rights, multiple sclerosis, environmental issues, and the American homeless, so I'll have to focus myself, but there's going to be a revolution you know, and Perry Farrell will be at the front of it and I'll be right there next to him!'

There was almost a whiff of the burning martyr about all this.

'Every time I get happy,' he went on, 'something fucks up. I'm not a pacifist, I believe in monkey wrenching, a theory which

Eddie comiserates with some of the fans who turned up for the Gas Works gig

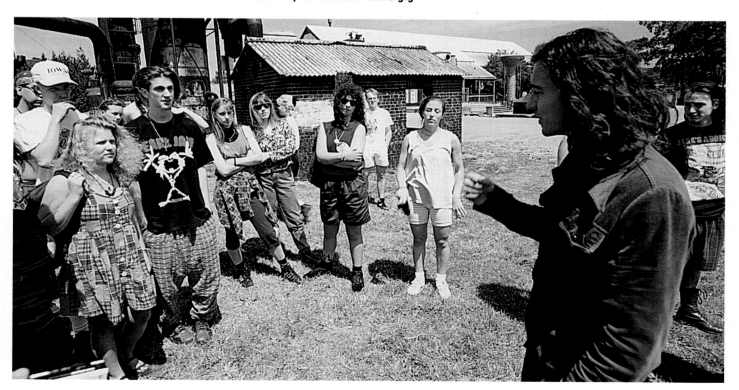

Eddie at London's Finsbury Park, June '92 (opposite) and the band in Seattle the month before

says you have to infiltrate and destroy from within. But I do value life. All of this that's happening to me now helps me deal with all the shit that happened to me before.

'It's like the negative fires of hell fired an interesting piece of art, and now it's cooled and it stands and speaks. It takes a lot of strength to appreciate life when it's shit. I've exposed myself to a lot of suffering, hospital wards full of handicapped people, and political issues, and it can change your attitude to life.'

Reading stuff like this, you wondered whether it wasn't all getting a bit too much for Eddie.

You also wondered what the rest of the band thought about the very public stands

Eddie was taking, whether they resented the way in which it was assumed that he was a mouthpiece for their collective views. When I met them in London in July 1993, I had a chance to ask them.

'We just can't get bogged down in trying to explain constantly that Eddie's opinion doesn't represent the band,' Stone said. 'And you have to remember, his opinions vary as much as anybody's. All of a sudden, he'll meet somebody and they'll have a different point of view than the one he's already expressed and he might listen to them and if what they have to say makes sense, he'll change his mind. His opinions on everything are changing all the time. I think all of us get flipped back and forth the whole time. You

change your mind and you change your opinion as you get new information, come into contact with people with new ideas that make you look at things differently. That's life, really.'

'There are some issues that we can all agree on, that are in a way so obvious and simplistic that there isn't really isn't a point of argument,' Mike McCready added. 'Like we all believe that women should have the right to have an abortion. But there are other issues that aren't so clear-cut, not so black-and-white, that we wouldn't feel quite so unanimously about.'

'For me, what the whole Rock The Vote thing was all about was just getting involved in the democratic process,' Stone said. 'It wasn't, like, "Let's elect a president who's into MTV." When you think about it, there are going to be various decisions taken at presidential level that are going be good for some and bad for others. No president is ever going to be perfect and no president is ever going to make everybody happy.

'All you can hope for with Clinton is that he turns out to be better for the country than George Bush, who was a disaster. Ultimately, the democratic process is a really effective tool and all it takes is mobilisation and people talking about these issues and continuing to vote, and if people continue to get more together and start to embrace the system, more and more good things will start to happen. At least, more and more notice will be taken of the way people feel about the country. All that matters is whether you are going to continue to be involved in the democratic process and keep yourself informed about what's going on as best you can.'

'But does that do anything?' Mike McCready wanted to know. 'Potentially,

Eddie at Lollapalooza II

yes,' said Stone. 'I honestly believe that Bill Clinton being president of the United States is preferable to having George Bush in the White House.'

Dave, who had been listening to all this conversation, had a rather more abrupt view on what we'd been talking about.

'To me,' he said, 'politics is irrelevant. Music is the most important thing in the world. Politics is just full of shit.'

You had the feeling, however, that these people would stand by Eddie and defend his right to say what he wanted to say about

anything and anyone.

'That's real true,' was Eddie's reaction when I mentioned this to him. 'I'm very thankful that the band has at least gone along with some of the things that I felt needed saying. You know, people's voices need to be heard. I'm in a position where it's like someone's given me a microphone with two really big speakers on either side of me. And they're pretty loud on their own, I can make a lot of fucking noise, get a lot of attention for things I believe in. And you add guitars and drums to that noise, and everybody's going to listen. You can really make yourself fucking *heard*.

'And I'll use every opportunity to make a point about whatever it is I believe in. And I don't think that's misguided because I don't think we're misleading people. We're looking out for *your* choice. We're looking out for *your* future, *your* freedom. I don't feel guilty about that. That's what I'm here for.'

June 6, 1992. Pearl Jam were back in London, appearing alongside L7, Therapy? and Mercury Rev at a one-day festival in

1992 saw Pear Jam scaling the peaks of stadium rock acclaim, from Finsbury Park to Lollapalooza

Finsbury Park, headlined by The Cult.

They went on stage in the middle of the afternoon for a wired, furious performance. Eddie went on with his long hair tucked up in some kind of velvet bonnet and looked immediately tense, oddly wound up. Even as his voice drifted over the crowd in a beautiful haze on the opening 'Wash', you sensed something here was amiss, fraught and just a little unhinged. Eddie had driven overnight to London from Europe, and was tired and dishevelled backstage before the band went on. Now, onstage, he seemed not quite there, more disconnected than ever. He was as compellingly focused as ever during the actual songs, but rambled weirdly between the numbers.

The audience, most of whom seemed to have come only to see Pearl Jam, were ecstatic. But even over the crowd's final wild applause, Eddie was bemoaning the gig, telling anyone who was listening that they'd

PJ with Soundgarden, Lollapalooza II

be better off coming to see Pearl Jam at one of their forthcoming London shows at the Astoria and Brixton Academy, where the vibe would be better. His frustration with this kind of large-scale outdoor show, with the distance it put between the band and their audience, was palpable.

THE EUROPEAN ZOO

A year later, when I met Pearl Jam in London just a couple of days after they played Finsbury Park again, this time opening for Neil Young, Eddie was even more distressed. The band had just come off a couple of dates in Europe, supporting U2 on their massive Zoo TV tour. They had played in front of over 80,000 people at a football stadium in Rome

and had not conspicuously enjoyed the experience, to say the least.

'It's not the same as playing in front of a thousand people or five thousand people,' Jeff Ament said. 'You can play to the person at the back of the crowd without wrecking yourself. But if you're playing to, like, 60 or 70,000 people, and you're still trying to reach those people at the back, what happens is you overextend yourself. You end up trying too hard and it gets to be not real. It's like theatre, or something. You're just pushing yourself to ridiculous extremes and not achieving a great deal in the process.'

'You feel very small,' Eddie agreed. 'And you start trying to compensate. But nothing you do is ever enough to conquer all that space between you as a performer and the people stuck right at the back.

'You know what offends me most about that situation?' Eddie asked. 'It puts the actual music in jeopardy. Even with all that amplification and loud instruments, music essentially is a very fragile thing and it should be protected. When you play these really big festival shows, just to get some-thing across, you end up exaggerating everything. And that really fucks me off.

'Maybe there are some bands who can do that, or just don't care. Our music isn't meant to be played like that. Maybe there are some bands who can do that, or just don't care that nobody can understand a fucking word they're singing and think it doesn't really fucking matter.

'But when I see a band I want to be able to look 'em in the fucking eye. And to be able to do that, you end up having to do things like put up big screens and have cameras flying around. And we're not ready to do that, and I don't know that we'll ever be ready to do that. Hopefully, I'll always have people around me reminding me that that's not the way to do it.

'You know, sometimes I'm at these big fucking shows and I think that what I'm being a witness to is the death of music. Because it gets to that point where it's not so much about music anymore, it's about visual spectaculars. It's a fucking circus. You

have to paint with such large brushstrokes you miss the fine detail.'

'It's not even brushstrokes anymore,' Jeff said. 'It's more like painting with a huge spray can.'

'Yeah,' Eddie said, maybe thinking of U2's Zoo TV extravaganza. 'It's just one huge fucking *cartoon.*

HITTING THE WALL

'Just tell 'em I'm really sorry, man. But we had to do it or there wouldn't have been a band any more.'

This was Jeff Ament on the phone from Seattle, explaining to the *Melody Maker* news desk why the band had dramatically cancelled their London dates after Eddie had allegedly collapsed with physical exhaustion at the Roskilde festival.

We know now, of course, that the band had hit a brick wall, that Eddie had genuinely flipped. At the time, this was an aspect Jeff tried to play down. Even through his polite diplomacy, however, you could sense that something more weird than he was prepared to admit had probably gone down over there in Denmark.

'The physical aspect of the last couple of shows we'd done was really missing,' Jeff went on. 'We were also starting to lose touch with what we wanted the band to be when we started. It's a combination of things. A lot of it had to do with not having been home for more than a week in the last year. It wasn't just the UK shows that went, we had to cancel a lot of European shows too.

'It was a hard decision to take. We spent the whole day after Roskilde discussing it. The thing that swung it was the fact that Eddie really lost it during that show. He was trying to get nearer the crowd, because the stage was 20 feet away from them. And he reacted really badly when the security tried to stop him. There was a real snapping point. None of us had the energy to deal with it on the level we should have had.

'If we'd carried on, I seriously don't think the band would still have been in existence by the end of the year.'

On the Lollapalooza trail: Stone Gossard with shaven head

LOLLAPALOOZA '92

You got there by catching the ferry from Seattle across the Puget Sound to Bremerton and then following the stream of cars, trucks and backpacking hikers all of whom were heading towards Kitsap County Fairground.

It was early August, a time of fine weather and loud music, and Lollapalooza '92 was four days into a 30-date trek across America. Lollapalooza was the brain-child of Perry Farrell, the outrageous leader of Jane's Addiction. In 1991, at the very height of their success, Jane's decided to do one last tour and split up. Farrell wanted their farewell shows to be something really special, a series of spectacular shows that everyone would remember. Lollapalooza would be the band's legacy, a vastly ambitious package of rock, rap and alternative entertainments.

Farrell's vision of Lollapalooza embraced more than just music. It would be a focus for what in the Sixties used to be known as the counter culture. There were any number of consciousness-raising events, exhibitions of painting and sculpture, workshops, poetry readings. It was a celebration, a cause.

It was a massive commercial success, too. At a time when the recession in America meant that even the biggest rock bands were struggling to sell out tours, Lollapalooza became the hottest ticket in the country. Farrell's unique vision had captured the imagination of a restless generation. They flocked to it in their thousands. By the end of the tour Jane's Addiction and the supporting cast – which included Siouxsie And The Banshees, Living Colour, Nine Inch Nails, Ice-T, Butthole Surfers and Henry Rollins – had played to over half-a-million people.

Pearl Jam were one of the first bands confirmed for Lollapalooza '92, the line up for which would also eventually include The Red Hot Chili Peppers, Soundgarden, Ice Cube, Ministry, The Jesus And Mary Chain and Lush. For a while, however, following the mayhem in Denmark, it looked like Pearl Jam wouldn't make it.

Eddie may have had the breakdown, but the rest of the band weren't far behind. After waiting for so long for something to happen, things had moved so fast for them they now needed to slow things down before fatigue turned into exhaustion and exhaustion turned into flat-out physical collapse.

What had happened at Roskilde reminded them of the sheer gruelling toil of touring. It had all seemed so exciting at first, but after a year on the road the thrill had gone. They had settled into a crushing routine, a

'I'll use my voice to speak for a bunch of people if the issue is hardcore and heavy. . . but don't come to me about a backstage pass'

predictable and cheerless litany of airport departure lounges, soundchecks, dressing rooms, screaming crowds, hotel rooms, bedraggled early morning check-outs from hotels that all looked the same, pointless interviews with people who seemed never to be listening to what you had to say.

It was travelling without seeing anything or getting anywhere, a blur of days and nights, in the air, long journeys by road, connecting flights to cities you could never remember anything about in countries you were never sure you'd actually been in and always, all around you, a babble of accents in languages you couldn't identify. It was the kind of schedule that could drive you mad, make you lose all sense of yourself and what you were supposed to be about.

They had arrived back in Seattle utterly shagged, but after a couple of weeks rest

and recreation, they started to reassemble their sanity and their strength.

By August, they announced that they were ready to go again. They had been booked for the tour before 'Ten' went super-nova, so they would be going on early, didn't have to carry the responsibility of being headliners, they could just go out and play, enjoy themselves. They'd also be touring with bands who were friends, like the Chili Peppers and Soundgarden. This would be a supportive environment. You wondered how Eddie would cope with it, but everyone kept emphasising that he was well again, that there would be no problem completing the dates, however gruelling.

Melody Maker's Andrew Mueller was at the Bremerton show and ran into Eddie backstage. He was shocked by Eddie's shambling appearance. Frankly, Eddie

Vedder was a mess.

'You okay?' Mueller asked him.

'No,' Eddie said. 'Not at all. Talk to me later, when everybody's gone home. I'll tell you about it.'

Later, Mueller met him again.

Eddie Vedder looked tired and hollow. He was still angry and upset about what had happened at Roskilde, the theft of his note books full of lyrics and stories. It had seemed like a violation, a betrayal of some kind of trust. He had been glad at the time to see the back of Europe. And then he had got back to Seattle and discovered that his friend Stefanie from Seven Year Bitch had died of a heroin overdose. It had put him in what he called a tailspin, a grim downward spiral of depression that he was still attempting to get out of.

He was still fighting the good fight,

however. During Pearl Jam's hysterically received set he had announced that in opposition to a new law recently passed in Washington State, that made it illegal to sell recordings that contained what were vaguely described as 'erotic content' to minors, he'd be hanging around outside Seattle's Tower Records, buying records for any minors who wanted them. This seemed to Mueller as good a way of starting a riot as he'd recently heard.

'Yeah, I know, and good point,' Eddie told him. 'I can't keep my mouth shut, I guess, and that's where I get into trouble. I mean, you know me, I think it's great seeing youth get out and come together and thinking they can change things, WHICH THEY CAN, but . . . whatever.'

Mueller recalled Eddie's last *Melody Maker* interview, with the Stud Brothers at the time of the aborted free concert in Gas Works Park, when he had said that he had no conscious ambitions to be a leader or a figurehead of any kind of youth movement, but would nevertheless be there if people needed him.

'*If* it's something important,' he said now. 'I'll use my voice to speak for a bunch of people if the issue is hardcore and heavy. But don't come to me about a backstage pass or . . . if I did all that, I'd have no time left for the important shit. Some people think singers can do anything. I know that . . . but leave us to the big miracles, yeah?'

Six months after he'd first met Vedder and Pearl Jam in Oslo, Mueller was struck by how much Eddie had changed, how his outlook had darkened. Eddie had been bright, then, optimistic and full of wonder. Now he seemed broken by events and Mueller wished him luck, thinking that he'd need it if he was going to pull through.

ROCKIN' IN THE FREE WORLD

At the end of September, with Lollapolooza heading into its final weeks on the road, Cameron Crowe's movie *Singles*, a feelgood comedy about the romantic complications of a group of twentysomethings in a Seattle apartment complex, opened across America.

At the University of London Union, February 1992 (opposite) and Lollapalooza (above)

Eddie, Jeff and Stone made appeared briefly in the film, as the members of Citizen Dick, a hapless grunge band fronted by Matt Dillon in a part allegedly based on Mudhoney's Mark Arm.

A soundtrack album was already out and in the US Top 10. It featured material from Soundgarden, Mudhoney, former Replacement Paul Westerberg, Screaming Trees, Mother Love Bone, Smashing Pumpkins, Alice In Chains and Pearl Jam, who contributed two new songs – 'Breath' and 'State Of Love And Grace' – which according to Jeff Ament had been inspired by Neil Young.

'They were our nods,' he explained to *Guitar Player*, 'to the energy we saw on Neil Young & Crazy Horses' 'Ragged Glory' tour.'

Young, of course, was one of rock's most illustrious mavericks and his basic guitar style and legendary truculence had become an inspiration for the new generation of American bands, who had adopted him as a kind of father figure.

Young had spent much of the Eighties in a wilderness of personal grief and artistic confusion. He had dabbled with electronic music, made a folk album, a rock 'n' roll album, a country album. A former political radical whose song 'Ohio', written in the aftermath of the shooting of four students by trigger happy National Guardsmen at Kent State University, had become a rallying cry for opponents of Richard Nixon, Young in the mid-Eighties had outraged many of his longstanding fans by appearing to support the aggressive republicanism and patriotic tub-thumping of the increasingly decrepit Ronald Reagan.

For a while back there, it looked like old Neil had completely lost the plot. But he had slowly and painfully pulled himself together, shaken off his depression and rediscovered the tumultuous power and raging electric majesty that had informed albums like 'Everybody Knows This Is Nowhere' and 'Rust Never Sleeps', but which had lately been absent from so much of his music.

His 1989 mini-LP, 'Eldorado', was a cleansing sonic exorcism that blew away the dead air of the previous ten years. It cleared the way for the 'Freedom' album, which opened and closed with a track called 'Keep On Rockin' In The Free World', a bitterly ironic state of the union address, that became a kind of anthem for the generation represented by Pearl Jam, Nirvana and their contemporaries. They loved Neil for his stubborn iconoclasm, his indifference to the fluctuations of his commercial reputation, for which he had rarely seemed to give a fuck. They loved him, too, for the sheer noise he was making. 'Ragged Glory' (1990) and the live 'Weld' (1991) were albums that took guitar feedback and distortion into thuggish new dimensions.

The empathy was reciprocal. Neil felt closer to this generation than he did to his own and had startled audiences on the 1991 tour during which 'Weld' was recorded by hiring New York noise terrorists Sonic Youth, themselves a crucial influence on

Eddie and Mike playing 'Masters of War' at the Bob Dylan 30th Anniversary show, Madison Square Garden, October 1992

grunge, as the opening act.

Somewhere along the line, however, he developed a special affinity with Pearl Jam, who had been regularly featuring 'Rockin' In The Free World' as an encore. Neil and Pearl Jam started showing up at each other's gigs, often ending shows playing together.

When Stone and McCready talked about playing with him, they spoke of him in awe.

'I didn't even have a conversation with him,' Gossard told *Guitar World*. 'I just looked at him on stage and he looks right back at you and you feel it. It's there in the way he relates to his band, his family, his land.'

'He smiles and there's this intense, total love,' Mike added. 'I'd never felt that sort of energy before. The first time we played 'Rockin' In The Free World' on stage with him it was like, 'What is this tremendous heat that's hitting me right now?' I felt like I was drugged out of my skull every time we played with him.'

'Here's this 47-year-old guy who just sent this chill through my body that lasted long after we left the stage,' Jeff Ament recalled. 'Before we even played with him, a couple of us went down to his farm, and he was sitting in his living room, playing his acoustic guitar. Two words came to mind and inspired me: pure and uninhibited. When he plays the guitar, it's instantly a part of him, and whatever is coming through is coming out of that guitar – and it's this pure thing. And he's fucking up and making mistakes, but it doesn't matter . . . it all sounded so beautiful. It's like finding the truth in yourself and just being able to speak it as it comes through you, especially to the people you love who are around you. But he could even do it in front of people he didn't know anything about.'

JUST PLUG IT IN AND PLAY

In October, with *Singles* still showing across the States, Eddie and Mike were in New York

to appear at the Bob Dylan 30th Anniversary show at Madison Square Garden.

Neil was there, alongside Eric Clapton, George Harrison, Chrissie Hynde, Johnny Cash, Lou Reed, Stevie Wonder, John Mellencamp, Roger McGuinn and Tom Petty, all of whom would be playing their own choice of songs from Dylan's vast and astonishing repertoire.

It was a stellar line-up, as these things go, and as these things usually went it was mostly pretty dull. Most will remember it for the disgraceful way the crowd bullied Sinead O'Connor into a tearful retreat. Musically, the honours went to Dylan himself for a poignant, desolate version of 'Girl From The North Country', to Lou Reed for snarling take on 'Foot Of Pride', to Neil for his typically raucous versions of 'Just Like Tom Thumb's Blues' and 'All Along The Watchtower', and to Eddie and Mike for what turned out to be a mesmerising acoustic reading of the early Dylan classic 'Masters Of War'.

At the 1992 MTV Awards ceremony

Eddie appeared on stage in what appeared to be a furious pent-up mood. He looked like the Semtex was about to go off in his head. Dylan's famous lyric had rarely been performed with such openly vicious candour. 'For threatening my baby, unborn and unnamed, you ain't worth the blood that runs in your veins,' Vedder sang with unequivocal disgust. He delivered the song's final venomous verse standing at the edge of the stage, looking like he was at any moment going to dive into what would have been a panic-stricken crowd. It was a marvellous moment, one of the evening's few genuine highlights.

Stone, meanwhile, was taking a brief sabbatical from Pearl Jam to record an album with a band he'd put together in Seattle with some old friends, including Shawn Smith, vocalist with a local group called Pigeonhed, former Malfunkshon drummer Regan Hagar and a bassist named James Toback who was taken on board the night before recording was due to start. The group originally called themselves Shame, but had to change it when in quite absurd circumstances an LA musician named Brad announced that he had held the name Shame under strict copyright and would not allow Stone to use it. Stone then retaliated by re-naming the band Brad (the LP they released in February 1993 would be titled 'Shame').

Stone's idea for the record was refreshingly simple. The band would go into the studio, plug in and play. They would tape everything and hopefully what then emerged from the spontaneous jams and improvised sessions would be shaped and nursed and edited into enough songs for an album. He was looking for atmosphere, not polish; emotion in the playing and singing, something that would have grown naturally out of the unforced inter-relationship between four musicians locked in a common groove.

The album was written and recorded in a mere 17 days, after which Stone took the tapes to New York to be mixed by Brendan O'Brien at Electric Ladyland. O'Brien was one of the hottest young producers in America. Over the last couple of years, he'd worked on albums by The Black Crowes, The Red Hot Chili Peppers, Stone Temple Pilots, Slayer and Aerosmith. His informal, off-the-cuff approach to making records made him a perfect foil for Stone, who didn't want to lose the rougher edges of the Brad tape in the final mix.

The results of their collaboration in New York were quietly spectacular: 'Shame' turned out to be slow-burning, languorous sensation that embraced taut dance rhythms, clipped Seventies funk and laid-back soul – Shawn's gorgeous voice pitched on these latter cuts against Stone's revelatory guitar work. It was at times like listening to Marvin Gaye singing with Neil Young cranked up behind him.

Stone would bring a lot of the attitude and approach that had informed the writing and recording of 'Shame' to the album Pearl Jam were scheduled to start recording in the March or April of the following year. He would also bring along Brendan O'Brien as producer, which turned out to be an inspired move.

Just after the record was finished Stone was asked why, with so much activity around Pearl Jam, he had decided to take on what they thought was the burden of making a solo album. This was the kind of question destined to test Gossard's patience. He was a musician, he replied. Playing music was what he did. And just because he was in a band didn't mean he couldn't play with other people when the opportunity came up. He relished the idea of working outside Pearl Jam. It was invigorating, gave him new insights, kept him fresh.

The band shared this philosophy. They were not shy about getting involved in extracurricular activities. It was as if they didn't want to waste any opportunity to take part in things, help out whoever they could whenever they could, keep things moving on as many fronts as possible.

Stone Gossard and Mike McCready

There was, for instance, the collaboration between Stone, Jeff, Dave and the rap group Cypress Hill, with whom they recorded 'Real Thing', for the soundtrack of a movie called *Judgement Night*. Calling themselves MACC, Jeff and Mike, meanwhile, would team up with Soundgarden's Chris Cornell and Matt Cameron, to record a version of 'Hey Baby (Land Of The New Rising Son)' for a Jimi Hendrix tribute album. Stone and Jeff appeared with American Music Club, on a version of AC/DC's 'Highway To Hell'. Eddie fronted the surviving members of The Doors at a Rock 'n' Roll Hall Of Fame induction at the Century Plaza Hotel in Los Angeles. He also sang on 'American Jesus' and 'Watch It Die', two tracks on an album called 'Recipe For Hate' by the seminal LA hardcore band Bad Religion.

COMMUNITY

When asked to contribute to 'Sweet Relief', a benefit album for the singer-songwriter Victoria Williams who during a tour with Neil Young had been diagnosed as suffering from multiple sclerosis, they cut a beautiful country-tinged version of one of her songs, 'Crazy Mary', that is among their very finest

recorded moments.

Pearl Jam seemed to truly believe in the concept of a musical community, the idea of musicians from different cultures and traditions playing together, like-minded people with a common cause, the breaking down of barriers and broadening of horizons. This notion of community hadn't been fashionable since the early Seventies, but there was certainly nothing cute or dated about their commitment to the idea. It was touching and noble, and it also produced some great music.

There was also in their sense of wanting to belong, of becoming part of an historical flow, something that suggested that they maybe saw themselves as heirs to a great rock tradition that had started somewhere in the delta loam of the Deep South as the blues and travelled through the country, where it got mixed up with the psychotic twang of country music, to the industrial north, where it continued to mutate and grow: into soul, Rhythm & Blues, rock 'n' roll and everything that followed.

Which brings us back to New York, and the end of a tumultuous year. On New Year's Eve, Keith Richards was booked to play a show at the Academy as part of Sony's end-of-year celebrations. It would be broadcast live, coast-to-coast, by the CBS television network, and also beamed live to an estimated 20,000 people in Times Square, via the gigantic screen Sony owned at the top of 42nd Street. Pearl Jam were asked to open the show. Eddie wasn't sure at first about such massive exposure, but the band eventually agreed to appear. They would do it for Keith, as a tip of the hat to the musical legacy of The Rolling Stones.

They played a short, explosive set – but what everybody would later remember was

Eddie's eccentric behaviour. He had come on stage with his long hair stuffed under a huge black stocking cap. There wasn't much at first that was odd about this. He had appeared like this before, usually shaking his hair loose after a couple of numbers.

Tonight, however, he was determined to keep his hat on. Much to his increasing annoyance, however, the fucking thing kept flying off. A few songs into the set, exasperated, he grabbed a roll of black tape and to everyone's apparent bewilderment starting taping the hat to his head.

It was at this point, with Eddie going out live from coast-to-coast, beaming down on the largest party in New York, that you began to realise how deeply troubled he had become by at least one aspect of his incredible popularity. More than ever, he had started to yearn for the comparative anonymity of the working musician, which is all he'd ever wanted to be.

Over the next few months, he'd hack off his rock god hair, let himself bloat up a bit on what you heard was a diet of pot and red wine. More disturbingly, he'd take to wearing a variety of masks – ugly, demonic, unsettling things – on stage, on the street, at the MTV Awards, where people thought he was drunk and not a little obnoxious, in photo-shoots for magazines. It would seem later to be a deliberate, even desperate attempt to disfigure his classic good looks, as if he was daring people to admire him less – in fact, *not at all* – for his appearance as his music.

You wondered then just how much he was beginning to hate the fucking sight of himself.

'A lot, man,' he would tell me later. 'I'm being honest when I say that sometimes when I see a picture of the band or a picture of my face taking up a whole page of a magazine, I hate that guy.

'Fuck, man,' he went on, 'I didn't get into this to end up as a face on a fucking bill-board. All I ever wanted to do was play music. Simple as that. I don't need all this other bullshit. But you can't afford to think about it too much, it'll just fucking kill you.'

Trouble Waiting

YOU were sitting in the gloomy corner of the bar in a hotel opposite Kensington Gardens drinking Lowenbrau when Jeff Ament walked in wearing a big grin and a couple of hats. Right away you wrote his name in the column that has GOOD GUYS written at the top. You had the immediate feeling that you were going to be on fairly firm ground with Jeff.

You were not so sure about Eddie, who followed him into the bar, shook hands, sat down and ordered another round of drinks without appearing to know quite where he was. You began to think later that this dazed, distracted air was something of a front, a way of keeping himself to himself.

For the moment, though, his distant, thousand yard stare, his reticence, whatever it was about him in these early minutes of your conversation that made him seem remote, not really *all here*, merely confirmed some of the things you'd been hearing recently about him.

You'd heard, of course, that since the success of 'Ten' he'd found it hard to cope with his own celebrity. You'd heard rumours about heavy drinking, that he'd become increasingly paranoid, prone to violent mood swings, unpredictable changes of mind and opinion. People you know were worried about Eddie. They thought he was trouble waiting to happen. They thought that maybe the success of 'Ten' had finally fucked with Eddie's head.

In short, you thought you were maybe going to have a tough time with him. He'd already declined to be interviewed on his own, which is why Jeff was riding shotgun here (I would meet Stone Gossard, Mike McCready and Dave Abbruzzese later), and you thought he might be withdrawn, surly introspective, mumbling. You were not immediately reassured by his appearance.

He'd put on a noticeable amount of weight and looked a lot heavier than he did the first time you saw him with Pearl Jam, at the Borderline, when he reminded you so vividly of the young Michael Stipe and you were transfixed by his presence and the holy rolling rock power of his band. His hair was shorter, too, in fact it looked like someone had been hacking at it with a pair of shears. With his battered jean-jacket, greasy T-shirt, battered boots and pants, he looked like he'd spent the night sleeping under a hedge.

And where did he get that voice? It was a sandblasted drawl, a parched, pot-smoker's croak, though don't ask me how I know these things.

The longer you spent with him, though, the more sense he made. You could imagine that his intensity might be hard for some people to deal with, and he was obviously driven, eager to do something with both his success and Pearl Jam's massive popularity. You hoped he was coping, that he wasn't getting fucked up, despite what you'd heard.

And consider what he'd been through in less than a couple of years. This was July 1993, and by now 'Ten' had sold getting on for seven million copies – five million of them in the US, where it had outsold Nirvana's 'Nevermind', and would shortly be certified as quintuple platinum. At the time of this writing, 'Ten' was heading back into the US Top 50, and had been on the *Billboard* chart for over two years.

MUSICAL STORMS

There would be further emphatic evidence of Pearl Jam's popularity in September, when they won four out of the five categories for which they were nominated at the MTV Music Video Awards, and where they stole the show from R.E.M. with a blazing set that climaxed with a version of Neil Young's

Eddie at Finsbury Park (opposite) and the 'Jam in London, Summer '93

'Rockin' In The Free World' with the grizzled old veteran himself on guitar.

It was a colossal performance, and it ended weirdly. Neil and Stone were wringing holocaustal noises from their guitars. Mike McCready was smashing his Gibson Black Beauty into his Marshall stack, which was belching smoke and electrical sparks. Jeff Ament was leaping through invisible hoops. Dave Abruzzese was a blur of hair and drumsticks. And Eddie was just standing there for the moment, head slightly bowed, his eyes lowered. He looked more lost and beyond it all than ever.

The musical storm raged around him, and it was like he really didn't know what to do. People were reaching out to him, but he had nothing at all to give them. He seemed to be preoccupied, in a space all of his own, where you might have had trouble reaching him. Then he suddenly seemed to come into focus again, and started smashing his microphone stand, raising it above his head and pounding it into fragments. When he finished bashing it out of shape, he smiled, and it was an eerie sort of smile, slightly deranged. And then he handed what was left

of the mike stand to the outstretched hands in front of him.

This was the kind of performance that reminded you that a whole generation of Americans, for whom Eddie had become a kind of spokesman, now hung on his every word. His songs and what he stood for had struck a loud and resonant chord. People believed in him.

'It's probably true that the first thing you hear when you listen to Pearl Jam is Eddie's voice,' Stone Gossard told me. 'And even if you don't totally comprehend what the lyrics are about for a while, or even ever, the first thing that strikes you even before you know what he's singing is the fact that whatever he's singing is coming from some place *real.* The thing about Eddie is that you always know that he *means* it.'

Not everyone was as convinced as Stone, however. Pearl Jam were not without their critics, some of them vociferous. There was an element among the British rock press, for instance, for whom Pearl Jam were still nothing more than shabby opportunists who hadn't so much leapt on the grunge bandwagon that Nirvana had started rolling as

Shabby opportunists ?

Stone Gossard at Finsbury Park

hi-jacked the fucking thing completely. For these people, Pearl Jam were just chancers, contrived where Nirvana were the Real Thing. The press loved this, of course - the two biggest new rock bands in America at each other's throats. It was a controversy fuelled by the late Kurt Cobain, who had continued his personal vendetta against Pearl Jam by publicly dismissing them in interview after interview as Seventies heavy metal throwbacks, banal cock rockers and worse.

This is what we're talking about when you join us.

'Thinking about it,' Jeff Ament said, determinedly polite, 'I'm amazed that none of us has ever said anything about *them*. I mean, the second question in every interview we did last year was, 'Do you know Nirvana, are they cool guys?' And there's only so many ways you can answer that, because none of us really know them. I've never had so much as a conversation with Kurt Cobain. We'd obviously seen them play, and I'd met Chris Novoselic a few years ago, but we don't really *know* them. So all we could say was, 'Well, we think their record's really cool . . . '

'But when you get asked that question more than questions about your own music, it gets a little tiring. You can imagine them being asked continually about us, and it's not hard to imagine it getting to a point where if you wake up on the wrong side of the bed and you get another question about fucking Pearl Jam, maybe you're going to say something that's perhaps not altogether complimentary. Whether Kurt meant what he's supposed to have said, I don't know. Maybe on a better day he wouldn't have said those things.'

'SEATTLE SOUND'

Eddie was keen to play down the rivalry, too.

'First of all,' he said, the soul of reason and understanding, 'I think any kinda quick success of the kind we had is inevitably bound to provoke some degree of contempt or hostility. I end up having difficulties with it myself.

'Like, I told this guy from *Rolling Stone*: 'Usually by the time a band get to the cover of *Rolling Stone,* I don't like their music any more.' Something's usually changed by then. They've become so popular, it's no fun to like them any more. So I have problems with success on that level and I can relate to people feeling animosity or suspicion.

'If I was them,' he went on, 'I'd probably be knocking the band, too. I mean, I remember hearing the kind of comments you're talking about and thinking, yeah, if people only know the band from what they've read in the press or the pictures they've seen of us or the way the record company was trying to sell the band – like in Europe, where they had all these "Seattle Sound" stickers that they put on the record – which is all the kind of stuff we don't have any control over, then I might have said pretty much the same.

'As it was, it made me personally examine the way we were being marketed and say, "Hey, let's try and keep ourselves out of that arena." Because I could almost see that these people maybe had a point.

'To me, that whole Pearl Jam versus Nirvana thing got out of hand. It should never have been made so public. But anyway . . . That's all been taken care of now, that whole relationship.'

And how was that accomplished?

'It's a personal thing,' Eddie said. 'I don't want to talk about how it was taken care of. It's fine now. End of story.'

At which point, I got a look from Eddie that suggested we move on. Which we did.

There was, after all, a brand new album to talk about.

The Satanic Versus

Against the Odds

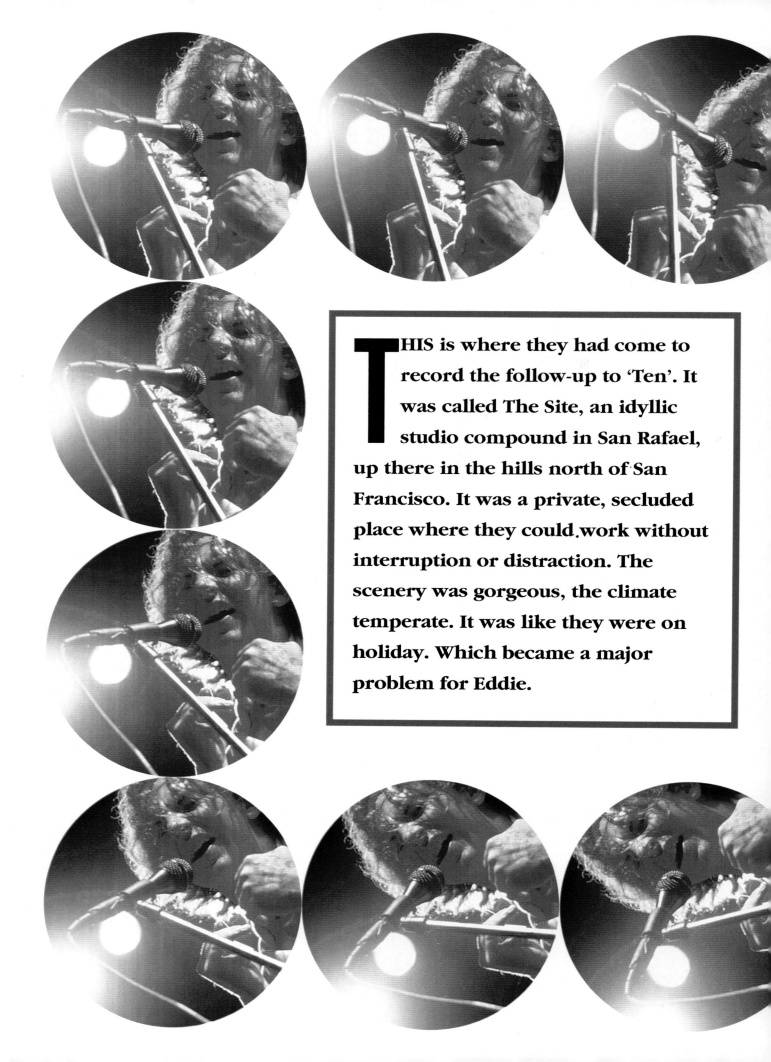

THIS is where they had come to record the follow-up to 'Ten'. It was called The Site, an idyllic studio compound in San Rafael, up there in the hills north of San Francisco. It was a private, secluded place where they could work without interruption or distraction. The scenery was gorgeous, the climate temperate. It was like they were on holiday. Which became a major problem for Eddie.

'I fucking hate it here,' he told Cameron Crowe. 'I've had a hard time. How do you make a rock record here? Maybe the old rockers, maybe they love this. Maybe they need the comfort and relaxation. Maybe they need it to make dinner music.'

At first the songs came quickly. They had spent two months in Seattle preparing songs shaping arrangements, everyone pitching in with ideas, and all the preproduction work was paying off now. In the first week of recording, they knocked off 'Rats', 'Blood', 'Go' and a slow, festering version of the unrecorded live favourite, 'Leash'.

Then Eddie started to feel uncomfortable, the lack of distraction at The Site became a distraction in itself. Eddie felt removed from the kind of everyday realities he used as an inspiration for his music. The atmosphere here was just too cosy, too cloistered. He started driving into San Francisco, walking the streets at night, hanging out in the rougher parts of town, sleeping in his truck, trying to get back into the mood of the songs he'd been writing.

Back at The Site, he left the luxury of the living quarters that had been prepared for the band. There was an old shack just off the main building that housed the studio and residential rooms that had previously been a sauna. It was small and dingy and exactly what Eddie had been looking for. He installed a four track tape recorder and a small PA system, and that's where he worked long into the night, on his own, after the day's recording sessions were finished.

They were soon back on schedule, and with Eddie back on track they were working quicker than before. Brendan O'Brien had set up the studio as if the band was playing a gig. They would be playing as live, and they were going for a lot of first takes, a minimum of overdubs, and mixing the tracks as they went along, rather than waiting until all the tapes were in before adding what they began to think would be unnecessary and superfluous finishing touches, those bits of fuss and texture that sometimes keep a band in the studio long after the creative process is over. It suited them.

What they wanted was the immediacy and excitement of their lives shows, which they felt in retrospect had been missing from 'Ten'. Of course, they'd only been together a few months when they made that record, they barely knew each other. Now, after a year and more on the road, touring themselves to a standstill, they were a much tighter musical unit. The music had grown, and as a unit they were prepared to take more risks. Nothing seemed impossible to them now. They wanted a record that reflected the band they had become, and everyone this time was involved to some degree in the writing.

On 'Ten', the music had been

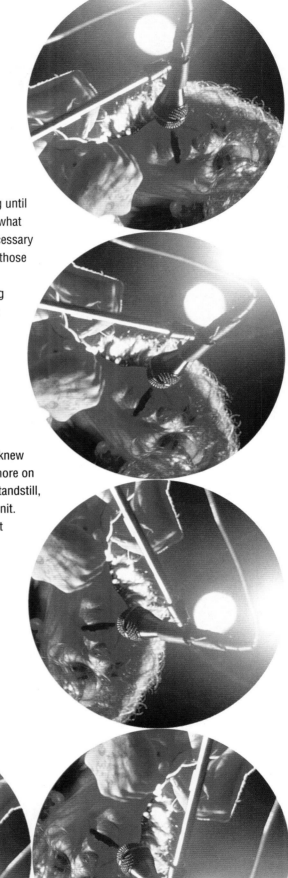

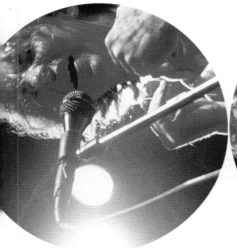

'I think there are some songs on this record that people will think are kinda weird. . .'

written mostly by either Stone ('Once', 'Even Flow', 'Alive', 'Black') or Jeff ('Why Go', 'Jeremy'), with Eddie weighing in with one solo composition (the incandescent 'Porch'), while two songs were credited to Vedder-Gossard-Ament ('Oceans', 'Garden') and one collective effort by the entire band (the final track 'Release'). On the new album, Eddie would still look after the lyrics, that was his turf, nobody else walked on it. But everyone was encouraged to contribute to the music, to the extent that Dave Abruzzese ended up writing key licks for what would eventually become the album's opener, 'Go', and the agonised 'Blood'.

'The trouble with a lot of bands,' Stone told me, elaborating on their approach to the album, 'is that they often go into the studio with a very exact idea of what they want a record to sound like. And that's the record they make.

'We didn't want to be that straightfor-

ward. I wanted things to get a lot more fucked up. I didn't want us to be afraid to make mistakes. I wanted us to try out as many things as possible. That way, you find out more about yourself, your band, your music. What's important to me is that we keep moving forward. The music should be changing and developing all the time. That's what keeps me going and that's what keeps the band going.'

After two months, during which they'd recorded and done basic mixes for nearly thirty new tracks, they were finished: it was over. They had an album.

YOU CAN CALL ME AL
THESE were some of the things they now thought about calling it:

• 'A Shark In Blood Waters', which was Mike McCready's suggestion.

• 'Paul's Dead', which Jeff Ament had a hankering for.

A video still from the MTV Awards show

• 'Al', which was Eddie's favourite for a while, apparently.

Why 'Al', Eddie?

'After Aleister Crowley. Some of the guys in the band are on a first name basis with him. Old Al. They talk with him before band meetings. He helps 'em come up with these theories that are hard to argue against,' Eddie explained, straight-faced, much to Jeff's worried amusement. 'I just thought it

'. . .that's really the only thing I could've settled for: an entire album of highlights'

Eddie accepting the MTV honours

would be kinda appropriate.'
When we met, it had been pretty much decided that the album would be called 'Five Against One', after a line from 'Animal'. They were all set to go with this when Eddie changed his mind. He was no longer happy with the title, even though the art work for the sleeve had already been done and the record was ready for release. Eddie wanted to call the album 'Pearl Jam'. Then he

changed his mind again. Now he wanted it called 'Vs' – as in 'versus', as in 'against', as in 'two sides in opposition'.

This is what it would now apparently be called. But what did it sound like?

Well, it seemed to me that anyone coming to it expecting 'Ten - The Sequel' was going to be shocked. Listening to 'Vs' for the first time was like having a gun go off in your face. It was brilliant, but hellish.

The rock grandeur that had characterised their debut had been largely abandoned. This was much rawer and stripped down, an explosion of bones and gristle. The band had also broadened their musical horizons. 'Daughter' and 'Elderly Woman Behind The Counter In A Small Town' were acoustic-led ballads, reminiscent of R.E.M. 'Dissident' rocked out like Neil Young And Crazy Horse. 'Rearviewmirror' and 'Leash' were fuelled by the classic rock burn of The Who or MC5. And 'Rats' was a really *big* surprise, a dank,

superfunky trawl through some murky and disgusted depths.

'WMA', meanwhile, was a piece of Vedder outrage at police harassment in Seattle, built around an avalanche of drums. 'Glorified G' was a caustic anti-gun rant that sounded like it had lurched off 'Exile On Main Street'. 'Go' and 'Blood' sounded to me like something from the demonic twilight zone of The Stooges' 'Funhouse'.

These were songs that constantly teetered on the point of complete collapse. They were violent, threatening, a collision of not always palatable emotions. Your first impression of the album was that it was chaotic, turbulent. You got the feeling of things not fitting together, a pulling apart, of an attempt to make sense of something too stubborn to explain itself.

'I think there are some songs on this record,' said Stone Gossard, 'that people will think are kinda weird and out there and

Eddie Vedder and Neil Young, both freeze-framed at the MTV extravaganza

maybe even completely fucked up and don't work at all. There are songs that are barely balanced in a lotta ways. There are some songs that are like one or two notes away from not working at all.'

HIGHLIGHTS

Is this what people were expecting from the band that had produced 'Ten'?

'I really have no idea,' said Stone. 'It's hard to say what people will think of it.'

'The thing is,' said Mike McCready, 'that you can't be defined by what you've done before. You can't make a record on the basis of what people *expect* from you. Making music isn't a marketing exercise. You just do what you do and go with it.'

Had they been inhibited by the thought of having to follow up a commercial blockbuster like 'Ten'?

'If you've got any sense,' said Eddie Vedder, 'you just ignore all that. You don't even think about it.'

We'd all heard by then, of course, about the problems Nirvana apparently had getting the original tapes of 'In Utero' past Geffen. Had Pearl Jam experienced any similar problems with Epic over 'Vs'?

'The record company weren't on our backs, if that's what you mean,' said Eddie tersely, visibly affronted by the suggestion. 'If anything, because of the success of 'Ten' we felt we could do whatever the fuck we wanted. And that's a pretty cool feeling. I don't think they were gonna *dare* try and tell us what to do.'

'We've *never* had a problem with the record company getting too involved,' Stone insisted. 'We have friends at the record company whose opinions we respect and we talk to 'em, as you would any group of friends, and what they have to say goes into the opinion pool. And we went swimming in the opinion pool once or twice, but I think if all five of us can agree on something, that's generally as good as it gets. We don't need anybody else's opinion.'

I asked Eddie what he thought were the album's highlights.

'Hopefully, every track is a highlight,' he said. 'I mean, we recorded twice as many songs as there are on the record, and they were all ready to go. So what we ended up with, everything on the record, that's what we wanted. That's really the only thing I could've settled for: an entire album of highlights. Obviously, people are gonna come to it and pick their own highlights according to their musical tastes. I mean, there's a lot to chose from on the record, to the extent that we used a lotta different . . . I dunno . . . different *colours.* I wouldn't say different *styles,* because I hate that idea of records

Neil Young (left), and Stone Gossard on the MTV programme

Eddie (right) with Neil Young who was recently dubbed the 'spiritual godfather of grunge'

where it's like, "OK, here's the song with strings. This is the ballad. This is the reggae song . . . " '

That way, you ended up sounding like a musical tourist.

'Absolutely,' Eddie grinned widely. 'Like, "I'm Paul Simon and I need a fucking career so I'll go to Africa or South America and I'll take their music, but I'll erase their words and write my own because I'm so fucking brilliant and cute." What *shit*. "You can be my bodyguard and you can call me Al . . . " What a fucking *genius*.'

' ' "You can call me Al" ' ' muses Jeff Ament. 'Do you think he's into Aleister Crowley, too?'

'Definitely,' spluttered a vastly amused Eddie Vedder. 'Paul Simon is the fucking Anti-Christ.

'Listen,' he said, warming up to this. 'I never usually say anything bad about any-body, so I'm gonna break one of my own fuckin' rules here. I just gotta say this. Man, I saw Paul Simon in real life once. It was at that Bob Dylan celebration thing in New York. He was in the crowd backstage, that's where I saw him.

'I had *nightmares* about him afterwards. He's fucking *scary*. Have you ever seen his face, close up? He looks like a premature baby eaglet that's just cracked out of his shell. It's really frightening.

'Of course, I'm really only saying bad things about him because I know if I ever meet him I can kick the shit out of him. I mean, he's so only so fucking tall,' he said, making a gesture that suggested Simon was even more vertically-challenged than you had imagined.

'Yeah, but what if his wife takes you on?' asked Jeff Ament.

'Who's he married to?'

'Edie Brickell.'

'Oh, fuck,' Eddie groaned theatrically. 'Then I'd be in *big* fucking trouble.'

CALL ME ANIMAL

WHEN Pearl Jam appeared at the MTV Awards, they were apparently meant to play 'Go', the opening track from the new album. Instead, they launched into a version of 'Animal', one of the most wrenching and emotionally disturbed songs from the LP, a seething, evil fucking noise, with a core of burning malevolence that suggested an impatience with what passed these days for humanity.

I asked Eddie who the anger on 'Animal' was directed at.

'I don't wanna talk about that,' he said blankly.

Was it too personal?

'Not so much personal,' he said. 'It's just

The MTV ceremony represented another step up the ladder of mainstream acceptability for erstwhile rebels Pearl Jam

. . . uh . . . well, some person at the record company said the other day that they wanted the vocals turned up. He wanted people to understand exactly what I was singing. So I told him what it was about and he said, "You're right. Let's leave the vocals as they are. Maybe we don't really want people to understand it."

So he didn't want to talk about it?

'Not right now. We'll just wait. Ask me about it next year.'

I tactfully decided to change the subject.

Talking last year about 'Ten', Eddie had said he was invariably drawn in his songs to extreme characters, people for whom life was usually a struggle in which the odds were usually stacked heavily against them. Was this still the case?

'Yeah,' he said. 'I guess so. I tend to be pretty extreme myself. I have a lotta moods, not all of them good. And the people I hang out with, the people I like, tend to be like that. I guess we share a background, which in a lotta ways is a background of struggle, of trying to make it. And if you're on that, like, lower level of society or whatever, you have to be more kind of resourceful just to get along.

'And it seems to me that it's always the most resourceful people that are interesting. I always get along best with them. It's like the best story-tellers are always cab drivers and the homeless. Because they're transient. They can expound a little bit, because they don't think they're ever gonna see you again. So they tell really good stories.

'Now you take people who are on a higher level in society, like some of the people who come backstage to meet us, people who've got the kinda connections that can get them backstage, the people who're doing pretty good, who don't need to be so resourceful because they've maybe got money and they know the right people – these kind of people, I don't have a lot in common with them I've found. You talk to 'em and you just get a

lotta small talk and a lotta pretty useless conversation.'

Was 'Rats' written about these people?

' "Rats" . . . ,' he began. ' "Rats" is just . . it's just using a lotta terms that are usually relegated to conversations about rats. It's not an anti-rat song,' he laughed. 'Don't even think that. I mean, what's wrong with rats? When it comes down to it, people behave a lot fucking worse.

'If we for once examined what we do as humans we'd realise that rats probably get along better with each other than we do. We're running around stabbing each other in the back, creating deals where those with the money keep the money for themselves and refuse to share it.

'They have deals, these people, where there's all these fucking people starving to death and they pay farmers not to grow wheat. What the fuck's going on? I mean, when in this day and age we can advertise in space or whatever the fuck they're doing now, are you telling me we can't somehow help some of these people who are starving to plant things that will grow that they will eventually be able to eat.

'No,' he said vehemently. 'We'd rather keep 'em hungry. I can't see a crowd of rats doing that to each other. I think rats are probably a hell of a lot more admirable.'

SHE HOLDS THE HAND THAT HOLDS HER DOWN

'Ten' was full of songs about the fucked up, the victimised, the dispossessed, the lost and the forlorn. You think of 'Alive', 'Why Go', 'Jeremy', the gorgeous, plaintive 'Black'. They struck the same resonant chords as American Music Club's 'Western Sky' or Red House Painters' 'Michael', hymns to America's deserted children. On the new album, there was a particularly harrowing song about child abuse called 'Daughter' that hauled you back over this troubled territory. 'She holds the hand that holds her down,'

Days in the life: the Pearl Jam scrapbook includes the Rock'n'Roll Hall of Fame gig when they jammed with the Doors (right, 2nd and 3rd from top)

Stone Gossard

Mike McCready

Eddie behind the mask at the MTV Awards, Universal City California, February '93

Eddie sang, and it was *chilling*.

'The child in that song,' Eddie Vedder explained, 'obviously has learning difficulty. And it's only in the last few years that they've actually been able to diagnose these learning disabilities that before were looked at as misbehaviour, as just outright fuckin' rebelliousness. But no one knew what it was. And these kids, because they seemed unable or reluctant to learn, they'd end up getting the shit beaten outta them. The song ends, you know, with this idea of the shades going down – so the neighbours can't see what happens next. What hurts about shit like that is that it ends up defining peoples' lives. They have to live with that abuse for the rest of their lives. Good, creative people are just fucking *destroyed*.'

'Leash' was another song that described the painful, regrettable rifts between children and parents who refused to understand or sympathise with them. It was a furious, angry thing, and somehow it was even more

coruscating on record than I remembered it from their live shows.

The song had been written about the same girl that 'Why Go' on 'Ten' had been about. Her name was Heather, and Eddie remembered what had happened to her with a fierce clarity.

'She was stuck in a home because she was, like, caught smoking pot or something,' he told *Spin* magazine. 'This is what they do

'Just ain't nothin' but he's got a great view'

in Chicago, in the suburbs. That's another thing I should have really said at the MTV Awards, I should have just went up and said, 'You know, as long as I've got everyone's fucking attention, will you guys just start fucking listening to your kids. Will you just please open up your ears and eyes and quit paying so much attention to yourselves, and just spend a little time with your kids, trust them, open yourself up to what they're going through these days?'

'Instead of doing that, they put 'em in a little hospital, which is a big insurance scam anyway. If the kid has any resilience at all, they'll go, 'Fuck you, there's nothing wrong with me. My parents are fucking freaks. My mom's a fucking paranoid freak, she gets home from work and sits and watches TV, gets all this information about teenagers from *Hard Copy* and then takes it out on me. I'm a pretty good fucking kid.'

'This girl Heather was in for two years, two fucking years, and she was one of the

'Maybe someday another child / won't feel alone as she does . . '

'After all is done, we're still alone. . . .'

'. . . .I won't be taken, yet I'll go'

smartest kids I knew. Now, Heather finally gets out, but the mom's still doing the same fucking thing, and threatening her with putting her back in the hospital. I mean, this girl was 15, 16 years old, she couldn't be on the phone after 8.00 at night. She couldn't do this, she couldn't go out, she couldn't spend the night at anyone's house, she couldn't do anything. It was after talking to her again one day that I wrote the song in the car. 'Drop the leash,' you know? 'Get out of my fucking face."

The drift on both 'Daughter' and 'Leash' seemed to be towards the idea that we somehow always betray the promise of what we love most, because we are somehow too thuggish, too insensitive to cherish it. And in behaving like this, we destroy what is most honourable about ourselves. 'Dissident' placed this idea in the context of a narrative about a political fugitive who's been taken in by someone who eventually turns him in to the authorities.

'The toughest thing is to devote yourself to a cause,' Eddie elaborated. 'And the people who do that should be praised. Because there are people who literally give up their lives for a cause. Like that abortion doctor who was shot in Florida. He gave his life to keep alive the freedom of women to chose to have an abortion. And it's something that should be their right by law. It's not as if he was doing anything illegal, although there

'I will be there once more'

are a lotta fucking people out there right now who want to criminalise abortion.

'In 'Dissident', I'm actually talking about a woman who takes in someone who's being sought after by the authorities for political reasons. He's on the run, and she offers him a refuge. But she just can't handle the responsibility. She turns him in. Then she has to live with the guilt and the realisation that she's betrayed the one thing that gave her life meaning. It made her life difficult. It made her life hell, but it gave her a reason to be. But she couldn't hold on. She folded. That's the tragedy of the song.'

GUN CRAZY

One afternoon in downtown Seattle, Eddie cut out of rehearsals for the new album to put some money in a parking meter. He didn't plan on being long, but the rest of the band were working on something that was going to keep them occupied so he wasn't in too much of a rush. When he saw someone waving to him from the park across the road, he went over to say hi.

'He was just this guy I kinda knew,' Eddie recalled. 'He's not exactly homeless, he just hangs out in this park. A lotta guys hang out there. There's some deals go down there, you know. Nothing too heavy. And I went and sat next to him on this bench and we started talking.

'I think I'd probably stayed at the rehearsal studio the night before and it had been a couple of days since I'd had a shower and I've got my old shoes on and I don't look too great, a little grunge on my teeth or whatever. And I'm sitting there with this guy who's of a darker colour than me, and along come these cops. Two of 'em. In Seattle, we got these cops, they ride around on their bikes trying to look cool.

'So here they come, they're heading straight for us. And they just ignored me and started hassling him. Compared to me, this guy looks as respectable as fuck. But they started hassling him, and that just blew me the fuck away. So I started hassling them . . .

And one thing led to another, as they did when Eddie got involved.

'I was just really wound up by it,' he told me. 'I had all this fucking energy rushing through me. I was *mad*. Really fucking angry. I got back to the studio and the guys had been working on this thing and I just went straight in and did the vocals, and that was the song.'

The song was originally called 'Policeman', and subsequently amended to 'WMA' (an abbreviation of 'White Male Armed', 'White Male American' or 'White Male Asshole', depending who in the band you talked to), and the way Eddie described it was pretty much how it came about.

'It's true,' recalled Dave Abbruzzese, whose colossal drum barrage drives this track like a train. 'Eddie just turned up and started belting it out. And that was the track.'

'Glorified G' sprang from the same traps, though here Vedder's outrage was mitigated by a sneering sarcasm.

'I didn't actually write that song,' he told me. 'I was at a band rehearsal and I just started writing down these things the guys were talking about. The band were having this conversation and I just took down the dialogue. One of the band members had just bought a gun. It was the drummer, actually. Ask him about it.'

I did, and this is what he had to say.

'I told our manager that I just bought a coupla guns and he told Jeff, and at rehearsal Jeff kinda blurted it out. And Eddie went, 'Whaaaat, you bought a GUN?' And I said, 'In fact, I bought *two*', which ended up as the opening line of the song.

'I think it's fair to say Eddie was pretty outraged. But like I told him, where I come from in Texas people have a very different attitude towards guns than they do in California, where he's from. Same with Jeff. He's from Montana. And that's where you have a gun on the back of the pick-up with a bullet in it, ready to go. Like Jeff's dad says, 'The best way to be safe with a gun is to always keep it loaded.'

'In Texas, people have guns to defend their land. Hell, I've had guns in my stomach a buncha times. But in California, because there's so much violence with guns and there are all these gangs, it's a completely different trip. I giggle my ass off when we play it live.'

'That's because you're a country freak asshole,' said Stone.

'That song is borderline nutso,' said Mike McCready.

'That song is borderline not working at all,' said Stone. 'It's *very* Eddie.'

Pearl Jam in London in early 1992

World Leader Pretend

THEY were the children of his republic, and he would have to speak to them. Eddie Vedder was on stage at the Warfield Theatre, in San Francisco. It was October 23, 1993, the first night of Pearl Jam's American tour. Outside, it was utter chaos. Touts were charging over 200 dollars for one ticket. People were crying and fighting to get in. There was panic and adoration in the air.

Eddie looked at the crowd inside.

'How ya doin'?' he asked. There was a pregnant silence. 'Because I worry about you guys, you know?'

The cheers shook the building. This was what they wanted to hear. They wanted to know that Eddie cared. That he was on their side, fighting their battles, speaking out to the world on their behalf. And there was awe and devotion in their applause for him. He had become a hero to them, a surrogate father for an orphaned generation who were looking for leadership, some reassurance, a new direction home. And despite all his protestations, there was nothing Eddie could do except offer them whatever he could that would bring them hope and relief and a sense of belonging, a reminder, as he'd been reminded by the music that had seen him through the worst of his own experiences, that they were not in the end alone.

'Vs' was out by now, of course. It had seemed a long time coming. The album had been originally scheduled for release in August. Then it had been put back to September. As every deadline passed and it remained unreleased, speculation about the record intensified.

There were rumours that Epic had been rattled by the album when eventually they were allowed to hear it. You heard reports that they had thought it was too extreme, uncommercial, not what they had expected as a successor to 'Ten'. That it was too raw and uncompromising. That the company were worried about it going head-to-head with 'In Utero', Nirvana's awaited follow-up to 'Nevermind', which was due out in August. Talking to people at Epic, you were struck by a palpable nervousness, a sense of apology for what they thought might be a record that would not match either critical or popular expectations.

Corporate anxiety would not have been calmed by the first couple of reviews in the English rock press. In a terse, unflattering review that barely mentioned the music, *Q* magazine thought the record's commercial chances in America would be scuppered by the fact for the first week of its release there it would be available only on vinyl. In yet another off-hand review, *Select* was grudgingly complimentary. *NME*, meanwhile, was predictably contemptuous. Andy Gill in *The Independent* was openly dismissive. Even some of the metal mags seemed unusually cool. Only the Stud Brothers were totally unequivocal in their praise for the record.

'This is a raw, festering fucking wound of an album, a brilliant, relentless passion play,' they wrote in *Melody Maker*. 'It's all we'd hoped for and one hell of a lot more than

Opposite and above, Eddie at the Berkeley Greek Theatre, California, Halloween night '93

many suspected Pearl Jam capable of.'

In the end, however, it didn't much matter what the critics thought of 'Vs'. The people for whom it had been made were the ones who would decide its commercial fate, and they were unanimous in their enthusiasm for what they heard.

In the UK, 'Vs' went straight into the album charts at number two, held off pole position by the simultaneous release of the debut album by popular teen sensations Take That.

COPING WITH IT

In America, however, the lid really blew off the kettle. 'Vs' was barely in the shops Stateside before it was breaking records on every front. In its first five days of release, the album sold an astonishing 1.2 million copies, smashing the previous opening week sales of 770,000 clocked up by Guns N' Roses' 'Use Your Illusion II' in 1991.

This made it the fastest-selling album ever released in America.

Pearl Jam were a part of rock history now, and you wondered how Eddie would cope with that.

You knew by now, of course, how rattled he'd been by the success of 'Ten'. You hoped what was happening to Pearl Jam

now wouldn't further mess him up, that he could maybe even enjoy it. Some chance.

On November 19, just over two weeks into Pearl Jam's American tour, Eddie was arrested in New Orleans on charges of public drunkenness after a bar room brawl.

The trouble began around four in the morning, after the first of Pearl Jam's three sell-out shows at the Lake Front Arena. Eddie was drinking in a bar on Decataur Street in the French Quarter with members of support band Urge Overkill and Jack McDowall, pitcher for the Chicago Whitesox, Urge's local baseball team.

James Gorman, a local resident, was in the bar that night and it turned out he wasn't much of a Pearl Jam fan. In fact, as he told Eddie, he thought their music stunk. Eddie's response was pretty phlegmatic. He spat in Gorman's face. Fists started flying and the fight spilled onto the street, with everyone by now piling in. In the ensuing mayhem, Vedder allegedly punched Gorman unconscious, while McDowall was knocked out cold by a bouncer from the nearby Blue Crystal Nightclub.

Vedder was the only person involved in what sounded like an ugly little scrap to be arrested and charged. He was released, pending further enquiry, on 600 dollars bail:

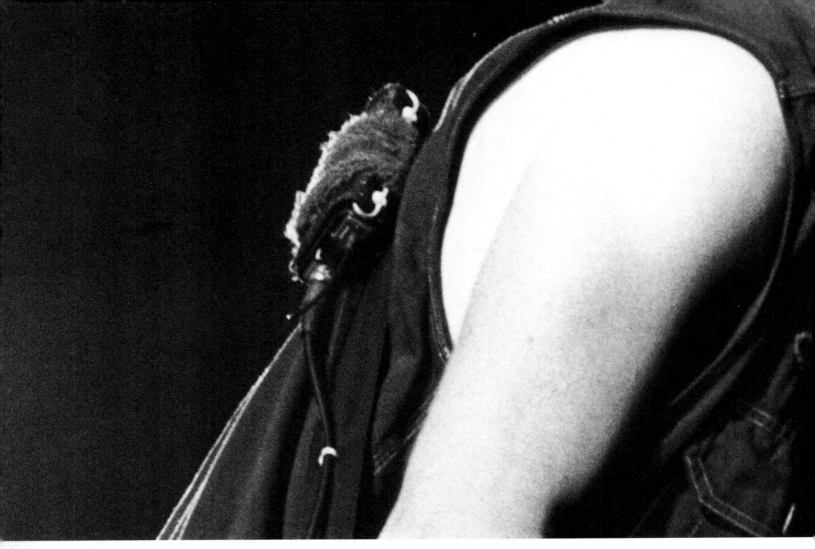

Jeff Ament: 'It's easy to lose control of your own career, your own life, your relationships, your friendships with people....'

if found guilty, he could still end up looking at a 90 day jail sentence.

Just over a week later, in Colorado, on November 27, he was in more trouble. Pearl Jam were coming to the end of the second of three shows at the University of Colorado when Eddie got into a row with security guards over the way they were manhandling the crowd in the mosh-pit at the front of the stage. He was later charged with obstruction and ordered to appear in court. Eddie was suddenly looking at the grim prospect of jail sentences in two different states.

Back in Seattle for Christmas, there was more weirdness when Eddie gave out his home telephone number during a live radio broadcast and invited calls from anyone who was in trouble and needed help. People began to wonder whether he wasn't losing the thread here, and speculation about how he was doing intensified in December when at the last moment Pearl Jam pulled out of

an MTV New Year's Eve spectacular being filmed at Pier 48 in Seattle. Pearl Jam had been scheduled appear on a bill that also included The Breeders and Cypress Hill, and which they would co-headline with Nirvana in a public display of reconciliation after their longstanding feud. The day before the gig, Pearl Jam announced that they wouldn't be playing. The official reason was that Eddie's voice was shot, that he was exhausted. Talking backstage on the night to *Melody Maker* photographer Steve Gullick, Stone Gossard, who'd turned up with Jeff Ament to jam with Cypress Hill, described Eddie as being 'extremely ill'.

It was a disappointing end to another mindbending year and you were left with the feeling that if only half the things people were saying about Eddie were true, he might still be in a lot of personal trouble. He was a worrying mess of contradictions.

He didn't want to be seen as an actual

spokesman, but he couldn't keep his mouth shut. He wanted to be anonymous, but everything he did drew attention to himself. People looked to him for help, but he was helpless. He had never merely wanted to be famous, but he was one of the most popular stars in America.

While he had never liked the idea of being a failure, if this was what success was like, you could keep it, Man.

THE DROWNING POOL

The success of 'Ten' had already shaken him because people had started to expect so much of him. Fans wrote in their thousands to him, and at first he had tried to answer every letter personally, spending long hours into the night at Pearl Jam's management office going through their angst-ridden and tortured correspondence. In the end, it just got to be too much. It couldn't go on. He stopped writing back, exhausted by the pain

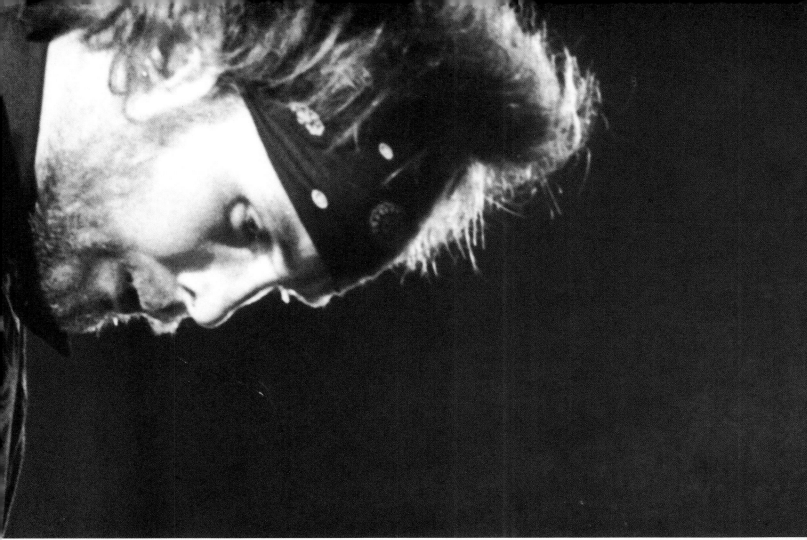

and grief he was expected to bear.

'They're writing because they think we have something in common,' Eddie told Martina Wimmer in an interview with *Musician* magazine. 'Something I've written is exactly the hell that they're going through. And that means for them that I must be going through it, too. They're expecting someone who's treading water to save them. But I'm the same as they are and what gets me through it is music. Other people's music has saved me in the past. And they can get all the strength they want from the music, that's where I get mine from.

'If they want it from me, there's nothing I can do. I can barely keep myself together.'

It seemed to me, talking to Jeff and Eddie in London in July 1993, that the fanaticism of their more troubled followers was turning Pearl Jam's success into a kind of hell. 'What *is* success?' Eddie wanted to know, fixing me with an earnest, baffled stare. 'Success to me is being able to play your music. I think some people want to be

recognised when they walk down the street, and that's success for them. 'Hey! Everybody knows who I am!' Big fucking deal. Some people want that attention. But not everybody, and certainly not me. And money only does you so much good. It also presents you with a whole new collection of problems, because now you have to spend your time dealing with it.'

'It's a great feeling, no question,' Jeff said, 'the fact that so many people have bought our record. It's an amazing thing to me. I can't say that I hate it. But at the same time, there's things that go along with it that are kind of hard to deal with. It's easy to lose control of your own career, your own life, your relationships, your friendships with people. Things start to change, and it gets weird, hard to explain.

'I mean, Eddie talks about not being able to walk down the street, down to the corner grocery store, without being stopped and hassled and asked a million questions about your band and what you're up to, and it's

true . . . It's like, you've maybe lived on that street for, like, five or six years, and nobody's ever said anything to you before. You had this nice little life, where you can walk to the store just like everybody else. And suddenly you're famous, the band's real popular, and now everybody wants to be your friend, like they've known you forever. It's then you begin to miss the way things used to be.'

'What we're not complaining about is being stopped in the street by people,' Eddie said, eager to clear this up, not wanting to sound aloof, unapproachable, an asshole rock star. 'Fuck, that can be like a real compliment, people just wanting to tell you how much they like you or whatever. That's cool. It's flattering. They're the people you can talk to, no problem.

'But the things Jeff's talking about, that's something different, man. That's what starts to freak you out. And I think the way I deal with a lot of it is by in a way not even admitting it's happening. Which is kind of hard

After the suicide of Nirvana's Kurt Cobain, Eddie seriously considered giving up the band

my own problems, let alone theirs.'

I wondered what Eddie's most typical reaction to these kind of fans might be.

'I'm just real moody,' he said. 'So it's a lottery. I can't tell how I'm going to react when someone approaches me. I think this may have something to do with the fact that I don't have a lot of friends. I never have. I guess it's because down the years, I've always been really dedicated to the idea of making music. It's all I ever wanted to do. Obviously, music is what drove me and what

'Music to me was like a religion . . . '

and makes me feel real schizophrenic sometimes. Maybe I'm just protecting myself as a writer, I don't know. But obviously there's something going on there where I feel the need to just deny it, and just be someone who picks up a guitar and plays and has this thing going on in his mind, which is music. So I deny all this other stuff, being stopped in the street, people pointing at you – 'Oh, wow! It's that fucking guy from that band!' Or you're having a romantic moment with your girlfriend of, like, nine years, and you finally get by yourselves somewhere and all of a sudden, even though you're, like, behind a tree in the fucking park or something, somebody comes from out of nowhere, and they're actually *running* at you, and they sit down and start talking to you about their problems, what they're going through, how everybody hates them, how they want to fucking kill themselves . . . It's a big fucking shock when that shit happens. You realise you can't escape. . . It's really unnerving,

man. It's like that really freaky feeling when you first smoke pot and you're very paranoid and you think that everybody around you is looking at you.'

The really frightening thing, it seemed to me, was when you realised that everybody *was* looking at you.

'Fucking *right*,' Eddie said with a slightly worried grin.

'That's just when things start to get frightening for me,' Jeff said. 'When people start looking to you for answers. I don't get half as much as this as Eddie does, but I still find it frightening.

'I mean, I'll talk to anybody, about the music, about us, about them. It can be really cool. But when people come to you looking for answers or want to know how to deal with their lives or their parents or their boyfriends or girlfriends or how to vote, I find it harder and harder to deal with. When it comes to them looking to you for answers, count me out. I don't even have answers to

kept me going, and I was just completely focused on it, probably to the exclusion of things like making friends with lots of people and just hanging out.

'Looking back, a lot of people I knew who were into music weren't inspired by it like I was. Music to me was like a religion. It was something I absolutely fucking worshipped. I remember going to see bands with people and after the show, they'd just want to get backstage and meet the group, hang out, do drugs, whatever. I'd never do that. I'd want to take the magic from the show, and *use* it.

'My thing was to take it home and use it as an inspiration, either write a song or write down a list of how to get my shit together, because I'd be *really* inspired if I saw some people who'd really got their shit together and were able to transmit this amazing inspiration, this amazing energy.

'I didn't want to go backstage, just to talk to these people. I wasn't interested in *them* so much, it was *the music* that meant every-

On stage during the late '93 American tour

thing to me. Who knew what the band were like as people? Who cared? Did it matter to me that Pete Townshend may have been off his fucking rocker? The fuck it did! What mattered to me was the fact that The Who were a great fucking band and they inspired me to make music myself. That's what was so fucking important about them. I didn't have any particular faith in them as people. It was the music I believed in.

'A lot of people live life second-hand. They have heroes they look up to. But in the end, nobody's going to do anything for you that you shouldn't have done for yourself. It's really important to me that people do something with themselves, the talent they have. People can be inspired by our music, but – hey! – don't come to me looking for answers. I'm not going to solve anything for anybody.

'Because when you get right down to it, when you get down to the centre of things, the reason these fucked up people relate to what I do is because what I do is coming from a fucked up person. Hell, I'm as fucked up as anyone I know.

'So the message is this: don't swim towards a drowning man. He's not going to fucking save you. You can only save yourself.'

WHAT DIFFERENCE DOES IT MAKE?

There was one particular track on 'Vs' that I kept going back to, over and over again, a song called 'Indifference'. Pearl Jam had previewed it at the first of their July 1993 Brixton concerts. They had ended the show with it. It was slow, beautiful and eerie, frighteningly calm, Eddie's voice glowing like the world's last sunset.

It closed the album, too, and after the mayhem and carnage of much that went before seemed like the quiet that might fall on a battlefield when the last shot had been fired and everyone was dead. Listening to it, you could see what was left of the banners and flags of opposing armies hanging like rags in the still, lifeless air. Eddie's voice on this track was the most impassioned thing you could imagine, aching, frightened and lost, full of doubt and dread. The song brought into question the whole idea of what one person could do to reintroduce sanity to a world gone mad, that had finally come off its fucking hinges. 'Indifference' confronted the idea of martyrdom, of making a stand in a world that might in the end be now beyond saving. It wanted to know whether fighting for a better deal was worth the effort. Was it great heroism or just foolishness, courage or mere stupidity?

It asked whether there was any point in even trying any more. Heroically, it thought there was.

'I'll keep taking punches until their will grows tired,' Vedder sang. 'I will stare the sun down until my eyes go blind/ I won't change direction and I won't change my mind . . .'

Relaxing during a soundcheck on the 1992 Pearl Jam tour of Europe

This wasn't particularly great poetry on the page, but Eddie *singing* these words was something else.

'He sounds not messianic, more alert and sorrowful, as if overseeing some endless crisis,' The Stud Brothers wrote in *Melody Maker.* 'The song's obviously about Vedder's personal conflicts but, like all great songs, when you listen to it, it could just as easily be about yours.'

'The way I look at it is this,' Eddie Vedder told me in London that July, as we came to the end of our interview. 'On average, we have maybe 50 to 60 years on the planet. And we probably have 20 years when we're a vital presence, when you can actually do something with your life.

'So what are you gonna do with that time? Are you just gonna enjoy it, not get involved? Or are you gonna try to do something to make some other peoples' lives better than they are, even if it means going through hell? Even if those people don't even appreciate what you're trying to do. Even if you're not even sure yourself that what you're doing is going to make any bit of difference.

'I go through cycles thinking about this. I mean, what do you have to do to remind people that one of the best things you could hear in this life is the laughter of a child?

'I'm always trying to understand what's happening in the world. I mean, what the hell is going on in Bosnia? Nirvana's Chris Novoselic has been working very hard to educate people and wrote a tremendous article in *Spin* magazine. And the bottom line when I talk to him is that there's no real understanding insanity. It's crazy what's going on there.

'You think it's fucking hopeless, that nothing can be done. But Chris is doing what he can, trying to raise money for the women's relief centres, for the thousands of women who've been raped.

'When it comes down to it, you can't turn your back on what's happening. You have to do something. Jesus knows, it's tough, because you never really know if what you're doing is going to have any effect. But what's the alternative?'

You walk away, pretend it's not happening.

'Can't be done,' said Eddie Vedder, like a troubled hero for troubled times. And that was it: Eddie had to split, Pearl Jam had a soundcheck to do, a show to play.

You shook hands, said goodbye.

And you came away from your afternoon with Eddie Vedder feeling that in a world of dull-eyed kneecappers, corporate stormtroopers and the blandly apathetic, this was someone who knew that even though you may die trying, it was still the only way to go.

See you in hell, Eddie, you thought as he walked away.